I thank my wife, Leslie B. Dougherty, and my in-laws, Carol and Alan Rea, for your patience and expert advice on the manuscript. The book is far better as a result of your efforts than it would otherwise have been. Further, I offer my thanks to those of my writing friends who offered their valuable insights into **Dungda de Islan'**. Their comments on that book helped to inspire me to write **Life's a Ditch**.

Charles L. R. Dougherty

The cover photograph shows the South Mills Lock at the south end of the Dismal Swamp Canal in North Carolina, viewed from the south side.

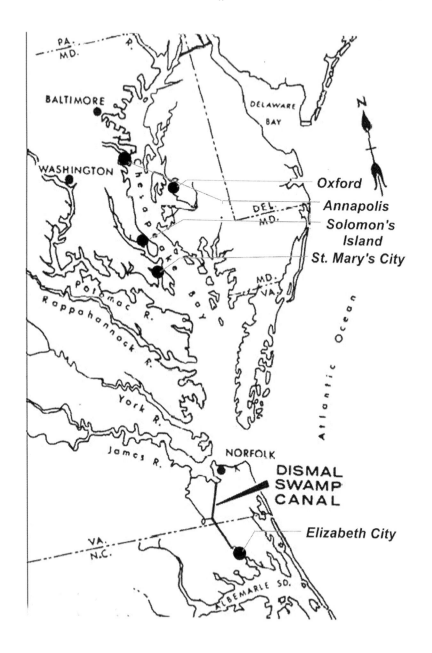

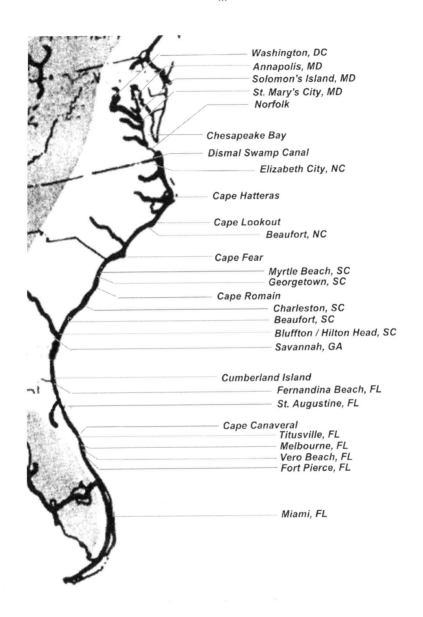

Washington, DC
Annapolis, MD
Solomon's Island, MD
St. Mary's City, MD
Norfolk

Chesapeake Bay
Dismal Swamp Canal
Elizabeth City, NC

Cape Hatteras

Cape Lookout
Beaufort, NC

Cape Fear
Myrtle Beach, SC
Georgetown, SC
Cape Romain
Charleston, SC
Beaufort, SC
Bluffton / Hilton Head, SC
Savannah, GA

Cumberland Island
Fernandina Beach, FL
St. Augustine, FL

Cape Canaveral
Titusville, FL
Melbourne, FL
Vero Beach, FL
Fort Pierce, FL

Miami, FL

Life's a Ditch

By C.L.R. Dougherty

v

Table of Contents

Prologue

"What kind of life is that?" the pampered-looking woman asked. We were standing on the patio of a waterfront restaurant near Myrtle Beach, South Carolina, waiting for a table, looking down at several boats tied to the dock. Her husband had asked where we lived, and she was stunned by our answer of, "On that green sailboat, right there."

That was 12 years ago, in the fall of 2000, and our lives are different now. We were in the early days of our first trip down the Intracoastal Waterway when we met that woman, and we really had no idea of what kind of life we had embarked upon. After that encounter, we spent a few years exploring the East Coast of the U.S., kept on a shorter tether than we had imagined by several family constraints. Finally, in 2004, those were all behind us. We decided that we had settled into a comfortable routine and that there really was nothing left to prevent us from leaving the States for an extended period. We sailed from North Carolina directly to the Virgin Islands, intending to spend around 18 months visiting the Caribbean Islands. We've been in the Eastern Caribbean ever since, but we still have fond memories of the time we spent exploring the East Coast via the Atlantic Intracoastal Waterway. One of these days, when our yearning for the open sea and distant horizons wanes, we look forward to revisiting those fascinating waters.

In 2011, I wrote a short, nonfiction book called *Dungda de Islan'*, about our first couple of years in the islands. Based on the interest and kind words of a number of readers, I am inspired to take a break from writing novels and tell a little more of our personal tale. Several people have asked how we built up to the two-week ocean passage I described in the beginning of **Dungda de Islan'**, and there have also been questions related to the practical aspects of cruising full-time for an extended period.

While I've always thought it would be fun to write about our early days as wanderers and the many lessons we learned, I knew there were a lot of books already out there about cruising the Waterway, or the 'Ditch,' as it's often called by East-Coast sailors. After the reviews and readers' questions I received related to **Dungda de Islan'**, I realized that a lot of the interest in that book has come from our reactions to the places, people, and situations that we encountered rather than from the particulars of our cruise.

This book takes a similar approach to describing our life in the Ditch. It's not so much about where we went and what we saw during our time in the Ditch, but about how we reacted and how our lives were changed by our experiences. Over the years, I've been tempted to write 'how to' books or articles about the cruising life. I started several, but I always stopped when I analyzed how many of the decisions about boats, equipment, and cruising grounds really had more to do with personal choices than with any absolute selection criteria. The personal choices are as endless in this arena as they are elsewhere and trying to enumerate them is fruitless, but you might enjoy coming along with us as we discover the answer to that lady's question: "What kind of life is that?"

Casting Off

We watched with a mix of sadness and anticipation as the classic Mercedes roadster drove out of the marina parking lot. The sale of our favorite car marked the end of our participation in the acquisitive life of America's upper middle class, although we were yet to realize how effective the severance would be.

Our angst was tempered by excitement at the prospect of what lay ahead. Our parting of ways with the American dream was voluntary, and we were thrilled to be embarking on the next phase in our lives. Our children were grown and starting their own adventures. My parents had recently died in happy old age, and Leslie's folks were relatively young and healthy. Our boat, although old, was well-maintained and recently refurbished. We were debt-free, and we thought that we had sufficient savings to see us through until a traditional retirement, so we decided to indulge our fantasy and go sailing full-time.

Since early in our marriage, we had shared the dream of seeing the world, or at least the parts that appealed to us, from the deck of our own boat. We had owned *Play Actor*, a solidly built, traditional boat designed for extended offshore cruising, for 13 years. During that time, we had enjoyed many weekends and holidays sailing on the Chesapeake Bay. We had reached our goal; we were ready to cut our shoreside ties.

After the new owner of our last car drove away, we strolled back to *Play Actor*, still tied to the dock in the slip where we had kept her since we bought her in 1988. The marina was in rural

Maryland on the West River, just a few miles south of Annapolis -- 20 minutes or so by car. We broke out a bottle of wine and made a supper of cold cuts and a fresh baguette we had picked up earlier at a gourmet grocery store in Annapolis. As we finished our simple but delicious meal, we sat in the cockpit and watched as dusk became darkness, rejoicing in our newfound freedom from the cares of life ashore.

It was early September, and we had spent the summer in transition from our shoreside existence to living on the boat. Most of that time we had two cars, and we had been traveling by car off and on, visiting family and wrapping up all sorts of things related to this change in our lives. In retrospect, it had not been much different from the two-week vacations we had taken over the years. When we were at the boat, we did the things we had always done: tinkering with the boat, running errands, taking off for a few days in a remote anchorage somewhere a day's sail away. The summer of transition had been a wonderful break, and we felt relieved that we were free of the last ties to our old existence.

The morning of the day after we sold the car, we realized that we were out of yogurt. That might seem insignificant, but everyone has something that they can't imagine doing without. In Leslie's case, yogurt is number one on her list; breakfast without yogurt is a grim undertaking for her. There was a small general store within walking distance of the marina, but we knew they didn't carry yogurt. The closest yogurt was to be found in a supermarket a few miles south of downtown Annapolis. It might as well have been on Mars. There were no buses in rural Maryland and cab fare would have been horrendous if we could have enticed a cab to come out into the hinterlands to pick us up. For all our married lives, we'd been urban dwellers; cars were fun and convenient but we had been able to acquire the necessities of life without one -- until now.

"Well, we may as well go to Annapolis. We didn't want to stay here anyway -- no need, now," Leslie said.

She was right. Our lease on the slip ran through the fall, but we had already told the marina that we wouldn't be renewing it. We had thought it might be nice to have a place to come back to occasionally during the summer if we got tired of exploring or needed to work on the boat. We unplugged and coiled up the shore power cord, a heavy-duty extension cord that provided our electricity. We stored it, expecting that we would be on ship's power from now on. We started the diesel and untied our dock lines, backing out of the slip and beginning our life as vagabond sailors.

We had a short, pleasant sail to Annapolis, happy because we had no plans beyond a trip to the grocery store. The notion that we could wake up each morning and decide how to spend the day was intoxicating, and we felt fortunate to be enjoying this new life we'd embarked upon.

Annapolis is a pleasant enough city, but we had never really liked it. Before this one, our visits had usually been on the weekends. In the warm weather, Annapolis drew crowds of tourists, and on the weekends, frustrated locals were added to the mix as they tried to do those things that most people are forced to do on the weekends. It didn't matter whether we had arrived by car or boat; the traffic was horrendous and downtown, though quaint, was packed with people.

The first thing that struck us as we made the turn into the Severn River on this approach was how beautiful Annapolis is when seen from the water. We realized that for three hundred years, the city has turned her best face to the Chesapeake Bay. Most visitors and a lot of locals never see that view unless they go out on one of the excursion boats. On our previous visits, there had been so much weekend boat traffic that we never noticed the lovely approach. It was a weekday, early in September; school was in session in most places. The tourists had thinned out and the locals were at work. After a half-hour of watching the city's waterfront grow larger and ever more attractive, we turned into the harbor.

We had our choice of moorings; that had never happened before. It was early for the hordes of cruising boats that flock to town every year for the Annapolis Boat Show, and the weekend visitors were at work. There were just a few boats bobbing in the gentle waves that made their way in from the Bay. We picked a mooring that would give us a short route to the dinghy dock and settled in to enjoy ourselves. As we were finishing lunch, the harbormaster's launch came by to collect the fee for the mooring. The deputy recognized *Play Actor* as a cruising boat, which flattered us, of course, as we were new at this. We would soon learn to spot the telltale signs for ourselves, but at that point, we were impressed by his acumen. In the unhurried quiet of the empty harbor, he stood in his launch and visited with us for a while. He and his wife, it turned out, were living the cruising life as well, pausing to work for the summers in Annapolis to stretch their retirement funds.

Paperwork done and lunch eaten, we dropped our rowing dinghy, *Curtaincall,* and went ashore. We found yogurt in one of the convenience stores, just a short walk from the waterfront. We were charmed by Annapolis and decided to stay a few days to explore, which seemed a bit odd to us, as we had lived less than an hour's drive from here for 12 years. As we walked the quiet side streets of some of the old neighborhoods of the city, we were surprised by how often people spoke to us.

We didn't just receive the curt nods that are often accorded to strangers, either. These people engaged us, stopping what they were doing to visit for a few minutes and make us welcome. They recognized us as visiting sailors, and Annapolis is the quintessential sailors' town. It has the same heritage as the seaports of New England, coupled with the warmth of a small, southern town. More than one motorist stopped to offer us a ride to wherever we needed to go. When we explained that we were just enjoying walking around, admiring their lovely town, they would offer a knowing smile and bid us welcome.

Being a tourist town as well as the state capital, Annapolis has an endless variety of fine restaurants, many within a few minutes' walk from the waterfront. We had lived our working lives taking many meals in expensive restaurants, often entertaining business guests, so we thoroughly enjoyed exploring the city's culinary delights, not realizing at the time that we were extending a habit that we would have been better off breaking.

We had lingered for most of the week, and as Friday drew near, we knew we should leave before the weekend traffic appeared. We had learned by then to catch the shuttle buses that ran to most of the places we needed to go that were too far to walk, like the mall and the grocery stores, so on Thursday, we took advantage of the buses to buy groceries for a week or so. Our plan was to head for the northern reaches of the Chesapeake, which we hadn't explored very often as weekend sailors.

Several pounds heavier and many dollars lighter from sampling the fare in some fine restaurants, we dropped the mooring line on Friday morning and sailed out into the Bay, watching Annapolis recede and assuring ourselves that we would visit more often in the future. As we merged with the ship channel, turning north to pass under the Bay Bridge, the wind dropped to a whisper, as it often does on the Bay. We started the engine and continued north under sail and engine power. As lunchtime drew near, Leslie went below to make sandwiches, leaving me to dodge the commercial traffic heading through the choke-point of the bridge's center span. We could have avoided that by going under one of the other spans of the bridge. Several are high enough for our mast, but I grew up around a working waterfront and have always enjoyed the chance to get a close-up look at ships.

I was admiring a freighter at close range when Leslie appeared in the companionway, worry lines creasing her face. "There's water sloshing around on the cabin sole," she said.

I had been around boats all my life, and by then Leslie had years of practical seamanship experience as well. But even a landlubber knows that the first rule of life afloat is, "Keep the water outside the boat." We traded places and I went below to see for myself.

Play Actor is a heavy displacement, full-keeled boat; there is a lot of volume below the waterline and her draft is six feet. That means that to have water sloshing over the floor boards, or as Leslie more correctly said, the cabin sole, there would have to be hundreds of gallons of water in the bilge. We have an automatic bilge pump which should have been activated by that much water. With the engine noise, we couldn't hear it running. We had been under power for less than a half-hour. With that much water in the bilge, we should have heard the pump before we started the engine. With the adrenalin flowing, I processed all this much more quickly than you can read about it. The inescapable conclusion was that we had sprung a massive leak to take on so much water in such a short time.

When I stepped off the companionway ladder into the main cabin, my shoe filled with water. I unlatched the floor board at the foot of the ladder for a quick look into the bilge. I didn't expect to find the leak in that particular spot, but it was the quickest way to see the water level in the bilge. To my immediate relief, the bilge was dry, as it usually is on our boat. Now, water runs downhill, even on boats. Everybody knows that, so our leak had to be above the level of the floor boards. The floorboards themselves are a couple of feet below the waterline, so I began frantically emptying lockers around the sides, looking for a gushing leak.

Everything was dry except the floorboards and my feet. I forced myself to stop for a few precious seconds and think my way through this. I decided that we must have a leak in our freshwater tanks; they are above the level of the floorboards. Although that created no threat of sinking, it would have been a serious problem if we had been hundreds of miles offshore. Fresh water is a precious commodity on an oceangoing vessel; you can't live long without it. Fortunately, though, we were only a few minutes from any number of places where we could fill the tanks, once I found and stopped the leak. Glad that the problem was less dire, I did a quick survey of the freshwater tanks and plumbing and found no problems.

It occurred to me then to taste the water that was still getting deeper, and I was dismayed to find that it was quite salty. As I started searching anew for a leak, it registered with me that the water wasn't just salty. It was also warm; much warmer than the water in the Bay. I thought for a minute and realized that it must be coming from the engine cooling system. I opened the inspection panel and looked into the engine compartment, seeing nothing amiss. I opened the hanging locker beside the engine where our foul weather gear was stored to grab a flashlight, and I saw a stream of water coming through a small hole for wiring in the bulkhead between the locker and the space under the cockpit. Relaxing a bit as I saw that the leak was really no more than a large trickle, well within the capability of our bilge pump to handle, I put everything back together.

Climbing back into the cockpit, I began to empty the cockpit locker that would give me access to the back side of that bulkhead. As I worked, Leslie and I speculated that one of the cooling system hoses in the space behind the engine must be leaking. Soon, I was peering down into the cavernous space under the cockpit, and I could see that the water-cooled muffler for our diesel had ruptured and was allowing the cooling water, which would normally be blown out through the exhaust, to pour freely into the boat. The warm, salty water had been running along a bundle of wires and hoses to eventually pour out into that hanging locker below, and thence onto the floorboards.

The flow rate for the cooling seawater is around four gallons per minute – not a threat, we knew. As we reached that point in our assessment, enough water had found its way into the bilge to start the automatic bilge pump. It ran a couple of minutes and shut itself off.

We weren't sinking, but we felt compelled to deal with the problem rather than heading off into the northern Bay. We still had a slip at one of the best working boat yards on the Bay, and we figured that would be the best place to sort out the problem. We turned around, glad to have survived the crisis, but somewhat chastened at the thought that this could have happened a long way from home, wherever home was now. At the moment, that familiar slip in the marina seemed a lot like home. We no longer felt like seagoing vagabonds; it was more like the time I ran away from home at age six and got to the gate in the fence around the backyard at about dusk. I realized back then that I didn't know what I would eat for supper, and my spirit of adventure deflated like a balloon with a pinprick.

Testing the Water

Having dealt with the leaky muffler, we resumed our plan to explore the upper reaches of the Chesapeake. For the previous 12 years, we had become well-acquainted with the area within a couple of days' sailing of Annapolis, and we had spent this summer revisiting favorite spots at our leisure. During our vacations, we had usually explored the southern reaches of the Bay as far south as Norfolk, Virginia, and we would be headed south soon anyway. We spent a few days visiting new places we had always wanted to see, but we were beginning to worry that the weather was getting cold and that we should begin following the sun.

We woke up one chilly morning in the third week of September and turned south from the mouth of the Sassafras River, heading for Annapolis. We wanted to make a last provisioning stop in somewhat familiar territory. We knew that following the Waterway south would mean we were always within relatively easy reach of grocery stores, but we also knew where to get what we wanted in Annapolis, and we suspected that our choices of gourmet foods might be more limited in strange places.

Annapolis was much busier this time; the southbound cruising boats had begun to gather for the Annapolis Boat Show, which always happened in early October. Conceptually, we appreciated that people embarking on journeys like ours congregated in Annapolis before the show to have work done on their boats and to buy all the wonderful new things that they imagined they needed at 'Boat Show prices.' Seeing the number of visiting boats was shocking, especially compared to our memory of our last visit. We did manage to find a mooring, but everything was crowded with people rushing around, frantically trying to get ready for their cruising adventures. We realized then that we were fortunate in that we had enjoyed the luxury of an entire summer in the yachting capital of the East Coast to get our boat squared away.

We took care of our grocery shopping expeditiously, but we did stay an extra day to do laundry. For the last 15 years we had both been working and we had a housekeeper who took care of laundry for us, so we were learning anew how to deal with dirty clothes. We had used coin laundries a few times this summer, but we had been driving a car then. We were on foot this time. We did find a coin laundry a few blocks from the Annapolis waterfront, but it was crowded by late morning when we eventually discovered it. We went back to *Play Actor* and Leslie sorted our dirty clothes into duffle bags.

We got off the boat early the next morning, dragging our several overstuffed duffle bags up a hill that we had never noticed before. It seemed that the laundry had moved a few blocks farther away overnight. We were the first ones there, though, so we loaded four washing machines. "Okay," Leslie said, "You put the detergent in while I get some quarters from the change machine."

"Detergent?" I asked.

"Didn't you bring it?"

"No," I confessed sheepishly, remembering the bright yellow jug sitting in the cockpit, seemingly miles distant by now.

"Oh, well, just buy some from the vending machine over there. The change machine doesn't work; I've got to go to the bank and get quarters." She sounded a little grouchy. We pooled our change and found enough to buy detergent and start the machines.

"I'll go to the bank," I volunteered, hoping to make amends for forgetting the detergent. I left Leslie settling down to read one of the shabby old magazines the place provided. When I got back ten minutes later, she was standing in front of the washing machines, engaged in a spirited conversation with a well turned-out woman; I noticed the beauty parlor hair and the polished nails. Her husband looked as if he'd stepped from the cover of *Yachting* magazine as he stood tapping his foot, frowning at the two women.

"I have no idea!" Leslie said, raising her voice slightly, which for her is shouting.

"Well, don't get huffy with me! Where's the office? I want to see the manager," Mrs. *Yachting* said.

"I told you; I don't work here," Leslie said.

"I saw you doing something with one of the machines," the woman said, accusation ringing in her voice.

"This is a self-service laundry," Leslie explained, apparently not for the first time. She guards her emotions well from strangers, but I could hear an unaccustomed edge in her voice. She turned away from the woman and walked toward me. "Let's go to the coffee shop," she said, eyeing the one across the street.

When we got outside, Leslie gave a rueful chuckle. Then she explained that the couple had come into the laundry and told her that they were on a boat, on their way to the Bahamas; they were in a hurry, and their laundry was in their rental car, parked around the corner. When she looked puzzled, they had suggested that she could bring one of the laundry carts to the car. At that, she had realized what was happening.

As we approached the coffee shop, my tall, slender, formerly elegantly dressed wife looked at her reflection in the window, taking in the ratty cotton sweater and worn jeans. I could read her thoughts; no one would believe that she had recently run a large, upscale women's clothing store in Washington, D.C. Brushing her salt-bleached hair from her tanned forehead, she said, "Okay, so maybe I do look like I work in a laundry. She was still rude, and I don't think they're going to enjoy their cruise very much."

****

Fall was in the air as we sailed south from the mouth of the Severn River, leaving the hubbub of pre-boat-show Annapolis in our wake, but we had a last stop to make before we truly began our voyage. Several of my longtime friends and coworkers had planned a farewell gathering. The venue was in northern Virginia, in one of the far suburbs of Washington. Understanding that we no longer had transportation, our hostess and another friend were going to pick us up at our old marina this evening and drive us to her house, where we would spend the night. Thus, no one had to drive us back to the boat in the wee hours of the morning. We were grateful for that; in our summer of transition, we had started going to bed earlier and earlier. The sun woke us at dawn, and we were usually asleep by nine in the evening. As we sailed down to the West River, we worried that we would be dull company for everyone.

The party was great fun, and the excitement was sufficient to keep us awake, in spite of our fear to the contrary. Our friends dropped us off at the boat at around noon the next day, in the midst of a downpour. The rain persisted for a couple of days, during which we read and did make-work jobs, like oiling the teak countertops, to try to hold our frustration in check. We were past the point of ready to go, but we just didn't have the heart to venture out onto the Bay in the cold rain; there wasn't even any sailing breeze to tempt us.

Finally, the day after Leslie's birthday, the rain abated. We rose early and took advantage of being in the marina to fill our tanks with water and diesel fuel one last time. When Leslie went into the office to settle our final bill, she learned that one of the ladies who worked in the ship's store was planning to leave in two weeks to make the trip down the Waterway to Florida. She and her husband sailed a boat named *Redemption*; their dinghy was named *Sin*. We enjoyed that, chuckling as we cast off our dock lines and got under way. With no wind for sailing, we elected to make our way south in short hops down the eastern shore of the Chesapeake; our stop for the night was a favorite, unnamed cove on the Wye River. The next morning, we were awakened by the honking of migrating geese, driven south like us by the unmistakable chill in air. We found enough breeze to sail down to Oxford, Maryland, an early colonial town on a low bluff overlooking the Tred Avon River.

The next morning we were anchored off the Strand in the delightful town of Oxford, which was one of Maryland's two official ports of entry in the 1600s. The stone building that was once the customs house still stands near the main landing. It's only one of quite a few things that haven't changed much in over 300 years. We had been here before, a few years ago, and we wanted to come back to continue our survey of crab cakes. Robert Morris, Jr., who financed the American Revolution, lived in Oxford, in a house that he inherited from his father. Junior invested all his savings in the Continental Army, not realizing at the time that he had invented the national debt. The family must have fallen on hard times, as his house had become an inn. James Michener, who wrote books about people eating, among other things, once wrote that the Robert Morris Inn had the best crab cakes on the Eastern Shore. We had to check that out, so we went ashore for dinner; we decided that Michener was right.

Besides sampling the crab cakes that night, the next morning we dealt with a vestigial problem from our former life. In our last mail packet, we had received a property tax bill for the entire year for the three cars that we no longer owned. A week or so after we got the bill, Leslie had called the tax assessor's office in Arlington County, Virginia, from somewhere where we had good cell phone service. While cell phone service is ubiquitous ashore, that's not always so afloat, even near civilization. After Leslie had explained that we no longer owned the cars, they had helpfully agreed to send us a revised bill for the prorated amount. That seemed to solve the problem until we walked by the post office in Oxford and realized that we wouldn't get the bill in time to pay it before the due date.

Mail delivery is one of those things that we had always taken for granted, but not any longer. When we decided to become wanderers, we found a service designed for people like us. There are enough full-time sailors and RV travelers to support a small service industry of firms that provide mailing addresses for a small monthly fee. They collect and hold mail and packages until you call for them, at which point they forward them in accordance with your instructions, usually in a fat parcel sent by your choice of carriers. We had been happily using this service for the four months since we moved out of our condo. The problem of the moment, though, was that we wouldn't be in one place long enough over the next few weeks to receive that revised tax bill and pay it before the due date.

After another call to the tax assessor's office and another lengthy explanation of our peculiar situation, they gave us the revised amount and all the instructions for paying by check without a copy of the payment slip. For a government entity, they were surprisingly accommodating. We rowed the dinghy back to *Play Actor* and put a check in an envelope. Once back ashore, we dropped the payment in the mail and resumed our walking tour of Oxford.

We found a kitchen shop that had Lexan glasses -- just the thing for a boat. We bought a set of four wineglasses as a belated present for Leslie's birthday. Just up the street, we had lunch in a little deli that was quite good. We couldn't remember the name for our notes, but it had a big sign out front that said "For Sale by Owner." We also replenished the chocolate locker.

Back aboard, we made supper of cold cuts, featuring fresh Parma cheese, smuggled from Italy by one of the folks at our recent bon voyage party, and a nice bottle of Shiraz to christen the new glasses. A couple paddled by in a kayak as we were finishing our evening meal in the cockpit. "Doesn't get any better than this," they offered, talking about the weather. "You're right about that," we agreed, thinking, "If only you knew how good it really is."

Familiar Places, New Experiences

After several chilly fall nights with temperatures in the low 40s, we were blessed with Indian summer as we started south again after our time in Oxford. With warmer weather, our compulsion to move south faded a bit, and we opted for a short day's travel and an early stop. We had always wanted to see La Trappe Creek, which branches off from the Choptank River just across from the historic town of Cambridge on Maryland's Eastern Shore. Cambridge, too, was on our list of places to visit, but having just spent two days walking around Oxford, we decided on the more bucolic setting. We made our way up La Trappe Creek, which is relatively narrow, with a high, wooded shoreline. We anchored for the night in Sawmill Cove, barely within sight of a couple of houses. We were struck by the peaceful surroundings and the almost unearthly quiet. *Play Actor* was the only boat in sight, although we knew that farther up the creek there was a working boat yard, the home of Dickerson Boat Builders, famous for their high-quality sailing vessels. After an evening with our books, we went to sleep early.

The next morning was warm enough for us to enjoy coffee in the cockpit as we considered moving on to Cambridge. Lulled by the surroundings and admiring the play of early morning sunlight on the fall foliage, we decided that Cambridge would still be there the next time we came this way. Sawmill Cove was pretty enough to warrant exploration by dinghy. As we reached this conclusion, we saw a family of five swans farther up in the cove. Leslie picked up the binoculars and stepped out onto the side deck in her socks, intent on watching our graceful neighbors. She stubbed her toe on a sheet block; her startled cry echoed through the early morning calm. The swans looked our way for a moment but went on with their business. Leslie watched them for a few minutes before returning to her coffee in the cockpit. She pulled her sock off, and we considered her rapidly swelling toe.

One of the things that we both enjoy about the boat is going without shoes most of the time, but one of the hazards of a sailboat is that there are innumerable small obstacles to trip the unwary. We both had enough experience with this to recognize a broken toe; it wasn't the first for either of us. I went below and returned with the adhesive tape and taped up her toe. She commented that it was just as well that we had decided to stay put for the day instead of going for a walking tour of Cambridge. We could enjoy viewing the shoreline of the creek at close range from the dinghy without her having to stand up.

After breakfast, we launched the rowing dinghy and put a thermos of coffee and some apples in a bag for a mid-morning snack. We spent the entire morning on a slow circumnavigation of our private cove, spotting several muskrats along the shoreline and deer back in the woods. The multihued leaves falling from the trees floated on the mirror-like surface of the water, resulting in a surreal appearance as the floating leaves mingled with the reflections of the ones still on the trees. The swans had moved on, perhaps farther up La Trappe Creek.

That afternoon, after a lunch of peanut butter and jelly sandwiches in the cockpit, we talked about our loose plans for the next few months. We intended to make our way to Norfolk, Virginia, over the next week or two, where we would find the official beginning of the Atlantic Intracoastal Waterway. We whiled away the afternoon in our secluded spot, enjoying the feeling that we were living our dream.

After an idle day in Saw Mill Cove, we were itching to move; neither of us had spent much idle time in our adult lives, and we were feeling restless without understanding why. We had spent 12 years cruising the southern part of the Chesapeake on weekends and vacations, and we had enjoyed several short visits to Norfolk in that time. Mile-marker zero of the Atlantic Intracoastal Waterway is in the Elizabeth River, right off downtown Norfolk. We were ready to be there. We considered our options. When we were on short breaks from work, we had often sailed directly from Annapolis to Norfolk; it's about a 24-hour trip for a boat like ours.

Now that we were retired, we didn't think we needed to push ourselves quite that hard, so we studied our charts, looking for places between Saw Mill Cove and Norfolk where we could stop for a night. We decided that we would do the trip in a few easy days, which meant we needed to head back to the western shore of the Chesapeake, where there were plenty of familiar anchorages. We elected to begin with two 30-mile days, stopping the second night at Solomon's Island, Maryland, a familiar spot from our previous excursions.

We had light winds and fog as we set out for our planned first stop at Hudson Creek on the way out of the Little Choptank River, so we were feeling our way out of the Choptank under power. We spent a quiet night anchored in the mouth of Hudson Creek, listening to the weather forecast before going to bed early. NOAA promised a good sailing breeze for the next day, followed by the advent of a strong cold front the following day. We were happy that we would be in the protected anchorage of Back Creek at Solomon's Island when the front came through with its stormy winds.

Typically, NOAA got it wrong, and we had to motor all the way to Solomon's Island. We were both a little cranky; using the engine to get from place to place was something we had done grudgingly when we had jobs and schedules to keep. We had been looking forward to having the leisure to wait for favorable winds once we made the leap to cruising full-time, so we were disappointed that we felt compelled to use the engine so much. We found the familiar anchorage in Back Creek crowded with southbound cruisers, or snowbirds, as they're called somewhat derisively by local sailors. At this stage, we weren't sure to which category we belonged. We wedged ourselves into the anchorage and began to make a list of things we needed to do here.

By then, we had discovered that life afloat was not as unstructured as we had imagined it would be, nor was it as convenient. One of our two twenty-pound propane tanks was empty; twenty pounds of propane is cooking fuel for about three months. We had been using the second one for around a month. We weren't about to run out, but we knew this was a good place to fill a tank; we weren't certain where the next place might be. We had always had the luxury of a car when we needed propane before.

Solomon's Island also had a good grocery store – the last one we knew about before Norfolk. And it was time to do laundry again; we knew there was a coin laundry there. It was too late in the day to undertake any of those tasks, and the expected cold front would preclude moving on the next day anyway. Leslie began sorting clothes into our duffle bags, and I took apart the frame of the companionway hatch, looking for a persistent leak. There was a forecast of heavy rain with the frontal passage, so this was a good time to stop that leak.

We were both finished with our tasks by dinnertime. Tired, we had a quick supper and went to bed early. It seemed we had just gotten to sleep when the cold front hit. The wind was howling in the rigging and the boat was yawing as she pulled at her well-set anchor. As we were dropping back off to sleep, I heard yelling and cursing over the sound of the wind.

Scrambling out of bed to go on deck, I checked the anemometer as I passed the nav station; the wind was gusting at 35 to 40 knots. I grabbed a flashlight and went on deck to witness several of the snowbirds' boats tangled with one another as they dragged through the anchorage. Fortunately, none of them hit us or dragged across our anchor chain. Once they had sorted themselves out and appeared to be securely anchored, I went back to bed.

Morning dawned cold and windy; we decided that we would feel more comfortable with *Play Actor* secured in the marina, since we expected to be busy ashore most of the day. While our anchor was well-set, it was obvious that others' anchors were not. As we watched our neighbors sorting themselves out from last night's mishaps, we felt a new sense of anxiety; we were at the mercy of other people's poor seamanship, especially in a crowded anchorage. We knew that in theory, but this brought it home. We finished our breakfast and moved to the dock at the nearby marina, glad that we could afford the luxury. This would also give us a chance to fill the fresh water tanks; something that had been on our minds anyway.

We excavated our folding, two-wheeled handcart from a cockpit locker and loaded it up with the empty propane tank and our duffle bags of dirty clothes. Two miles up the road, we were grateful for the cart. I helped Leslie get the laundry started and took the propane tank to the local gas station for a fill-up. When I got back to the laundry, we went next door for a cup of coffee. We sat on stools looking out the window, watching the foot traffic.

We soon figured out that most of the people we saw were fellow cruisers. The boat show in Annapolis was over, and the herd was moving south. We observed that they seemed to run in packs; we rarely saw single couples, and never individuals of the species. As we went back to the laundry, we were able to eavesdrop a bit, and it became clear to us that these people all knew one another. Further, most of them seemed new at this, sporting the latest, must-have cruising gear: hats, foul weather jackets, backpacks, and so forth, all freshly acquired at the boat show.

We continued to see them when we got back to the boat; we had a nice view of the crowded anchorage, and as we rested from our morning's exertions, we watched the dinghy traffic as the people visited from boat to boat. We noticed that a fair percentage of the boats were Canadian-flagged, and that the Canadians seemed to visit among themselves, as did the American-flagged boats. We started checking the hailing ports on the U.S. flagged boats, and saw that many were from the Great Lakes, and quite a few of the others were from the northeastern U.S.

We realized that these people had been in one another's company for quite a while, and we began to feel a little bit left out. We aren't party animals, and we had been enjoying our solitude over the summer, but it was sort of like the experience of going to a party where everyone knew everyone else and we were the only outsiders. Perhaps, we thought, it was because they had seen our Virginia hailing port painted across the stern and took us for local boaters. Then we realized that it was simply that we hadn't been among them. They had spent the summer traveling together, getting to the Chesapeake, while we had enjoyed the summer cruising local waters. We considered whether we wanted to be part of the crowd, and decided to take it slowly and stay to ourselves for a while. As I said, we aren't really party people.

We stowed our clean clothes, had a quick lunch, and went to the grocery store that we remembered from previous visits over the years. We were pleasantly surprised that the store had undergone a makeover and was quite upscale. When we mentioned it to the cashier, she smiled and confessed that it was a response to competition from the new chain grocery store that had opened just a bit farther up the road, accompanied by a new shopping center. Solomon's Island had become a boom town since we were there last.

We dragged our groceries back to the boat, thoroughly tired by now, and put them away. After a couple of hours of rest, we used my recent birthday as an excuse to visit the marina's excellent but expensive restaurant for dinner. Back aboard the boat, we took advantage of being able to plug into the marina's shore power and ran our electric heaters, enjoying reading in our snug cabin as the cold winds howled through the rigging, glad again that we could afford the luxury of staying in a marina on such a nasty night. As we listened to the weather forecast before going to bed, we realized that we would be here for a few days before we could move south in comfort.

The next morning, we had a leisurely breakfast, in no hurry to leave our cocoon of warmth. We were both tired from the previous day's activities, and we mused aloud about how much time it took to accomplish mundane tasks in our new life. I remarked that grocery shopping and laundry had consumed a whole day. Leslie pointed out that the same tasks had taken us four days in Annapolis a month ago. We had improved our efficiency, or maybe Solomon's Island was an easier place to get things done.

We eventually got dressed and went to the Calvert Marine Museum. We were impressed with the changes that had taken place since our last visit; we had been longtime contributors to the museum, and we were pleased to see that our small donations had been well used. After lunch, we spent the afternoon snuggled up, reading and resting, hoping for a break in the weather tomorrow so we could move farther south. We were tired of cold weather.

That evening, we listened to the weather. To our disappointment, we learned that we had another day of enforced idleness ahead of us. The wind had shifted, raising a chop in the harbor, and we were experiencing a jerky, uncomfortable motion tied to the dock. The next morning, we took the dinghy up the creek and discovered that there was room to anchor well beyond the crowded spot where all the other cruising boats were congregated. We wondered why no one was there, and then realized that the chart erroneously showed very shallow water in the area. We settled up with the marina and moved *Play Actor* to our new spot, discovering that not only was there sufficient depth to anchor, but that the trees and high bluffs broke the wind. The boat was riding more comfortably than she had been at the dock last night, but we realized we would miss the electric heat. We cleaned and prepared our diesel heater for use, just in case, but by late afternoon, the wind abated, and it was pleasantly warm.

Joining the Southerly Migration

We were up and away at dawn, along with a few of the snowbirds, just like the migrating geese at sunrise. There was a perfect forecast for sailing south; we were expecting a 15-knot wind from the west. We left the Solomon's Island entrance, easing out into the Patuxent River, disappointed to find no wind. We turned our bow to the east and headed for the Bay, diesel rumbling happily. An hour later, we were clear of the Patuxent, and the breeze had filled in. We were enjoying a glorious sail, making between six and seven knots in the direction we wanted to go. Finally, we were sailing, enjoying the silence as *Play Actor* sliced easily through the slight wind chop that ruffled the surface of the Chesapeake. It would have been a perfect morning if it had been just a little warmer, but it was grand to be on our way at last. We enjoyed our thermos of coffee, glad that we were dressed warmly.

By the time we finished the coffee, the wind had built to 20 knots, and *Play Actor* was overpowered, so we took the first reef in the mainsail. With the reduction in sail area, the boat stood up again, shaking the water from her lee rail, which had been submerged during the gusts. We looked around, wondering where the rest of the crowd had gone. Was it possible that we had outrun them? Not likely, we thought, although this is the perfect day for our heavy displacement, full-keeled boat.

Within four hours, we turned up into the mouth of the Potomac River, headed for St. Mary's City, Maryland's first capital, where we planned to spend the night. The wind had clocked to the northwest and built in strength; it was now blowing close to 30 knots, straight from our destination. Oh, well, we wanted to sail, so sail we would. We beat into the wind, changing tacks frequently to work our way up the Potomac for several hours, occasionally dipping the end of the boom into the water. We were over-canvassed again, but the water was flat, we were tired, and we were almost there, so we decided not to reduce sail. Soon, we turned up into the St. Mary's River where we were protected from the wind. We dropped the sails, started the diesel, and motored into the anchorage a few minutes later.

The anchorage at St. Mary's City is a fine natural harbor; no doubt it's why the original colonists built their capital here. The basin is almost a mile wide, completely protected from all directions, and 15 to 20 feet deep from shore to shore. We were sharing it with one other boat. We wondered again where the crowd of snowbirds went. Maybe they heard a later forecast than the one we listened to and turned around and stayed in Solomon's Island. NOAA at this point had a small craft advisory out for the Chesapeake, with strong winds predicted through the next night, so we decided to stay put for a day.

Checking our logbook, we learned that we last visited St. Mary's City in 1992. After reading the notes, we remembered that trip well; we had been caught out on the Bay in a full gale, with 45-knot winds from the north as we tried to go, you guessed it, north. After a couple of tacks across the Bay, we realized that we were making better speed than the container ship that was plowing north up the Bay. Although we had been making over five knots through the water, in several hours we had gotten ahead of the ship and still only gained a few miles in the direction we were traveling. We had turned and run into St. Mary's City for shelter that time, and we were happy enough to spend an extra day here on this trip.

There's not much ashore in St. Mary's City. St. Mary's College, a small, public, liberal arts college, is the main attraction. There is a replica of the 1634 State House, built in 1934 to celebrate the 300th anniversary of Maryland's founding, and there were a few archaeological sites which we visited years ago. St. Mary's City was the center of government for the colony from 1634 until 1695, when the English Crown took over the colony from the Calvert family and moved the capital to Annapolis. We had enjoyed visiting back in 1992, and we looked forward to seeing what had changed in the eight years since then.

We cooked a hot meal of pasta, enjoyed a little wine from our cellar (the bilge) and went to sleep early, tired from the boisterous sail.

****

We were surprised at how much St. Mary's City had changed. On our earlier visits, it had been possible to step into the archaeological digs and chat with the people working them. Now the active sites were roped off, and there were a number of reconstructions and partial reconstructions. Drama students from the college were attired in period costumes and served as docents; we could see that in a few more years, St. Mary's City might rival Colonial Williamsburg as a tourist attraction, although its location is a bit off the beaten path.

We enjoyed our day, having lunch at the student union and stopping to go aboard the *Dove* on our way back to *Play Actor*. The

Dove is a recently constructed replica of one of the two ships that brought the first colonists to Maryland. We were struck by how small she was, given the number of passengers and crew she had carried. The replica was a magnificent example of the shipwright's art, authentic as best we could tell, except for the twin diesel engines hiding in the hold.

That evening, we lit the heater and read, pausing every so often to reflect on how luxurious our accommodations were compared to those of the original seaborne visitors to St. Mary's City.

****

Four days later, after a series of short, overnight stops in anchorages just off the Bay, we pulled into Mill Creek at Hampton Roads, Virginia. We were in sight of Norfolk; it's just across the broad area where the James River and the Elizabeth River flow into the Chesapeake. Mill Creek is a convenient anchorage that offers protection from the choppy seas at the mouth of the Bay. We had made arrangements to pick up several months' worth of Leslie's medication at a pharmacy in Norfolk, and the order wouldn't be ready for a few days yet, so we had time to kill.

We realized as we were leaving the northern Bay a few weeks ago that we should stock up on her medication, as filling prescriptions in states where her doctor wasn't licensed might be a problem. Norfolk would be our southernmost stop in Virginia, and we were planning to spend the winter in the Bahamas, where it would be difficult or impossible to find her medicine, with or without a valid prescription. When we placed the order with the pharmacy by phone, it had been a little difficult to make the pharmacist understand what we were doing. He had told us that most insurance wouldn't allow more than a 90-day supply. Leslie had explained that we didn't have insurance, and that we would be paying for the medication. He was stunned; the amount of money was several thousand dollars for several months' worth of her prescriptions.

We had anticipated the expense and the potential difficulty, but this was the first time that one or the other of us had not had insurance to help defray the expense. The pharmacist had accepted a deposit over the telephone via credit card. Early in our planning, we recognized that Leslie's need for medication would be a constraint on our travels, as well as a significant fixed expense in our budget, but actually dealing with the problem was sobering for both of us.

Meanwhile, we made arrangements to spend a couple of nights in the Newport News Municipal Marina, just a short distance up the James River. We wanted to see the Mariner's Museum in Newport News, and we were within a few miles of Norfolk, across protected water, so weather was not a factor in our immediate travel plans. We secured *Play Actor* in the marina at around 10:00 a.m. There was a sketch map in one of our guide books that showed Newport News, and it appeared that the Museum was just on the outskirts of town. The marina manager confirmed that it was only a few minutes away. We were both fit, having spent years running several miles a day, so we declined his offer to call a cab for us, and we took off walking. About an hour and a half later, we arrived. The Museum was well out in the country, and there was nowhere to buy lunch nearby. Famished, we made do with snack food from the vending machines in the canteen at the museum. Although we were tired and hungry, we thoroughly enjoyed the exhibits. We left in time to make the hike back to the boat in the waning daylight, had sandwiches aboard, and crashed, exhausted.

We spent the next day walking around Newport News, not venturing too far from the comforts of home, We had learned our lesson; the sketch maps in tourist brochures would be of little use to us without that ubiquitous American conveyance, a car. That evening over dinner aboard, we talked about our changing expectations.

Approaching Norfolk

We were excited at the prospect that tomorrow we would be in Norfolk. We had kept *Play Actor* on the Chesapeake as long as we had owned her, and Norfolk was the southern limit of our travels so far. We had always enjoyed visiting the city; everything a vacationing boater needs is within walking distance of the waterfront. But it was beginning to register with us that we weren't on vacation. We had moved out of our condo in May, and now it was mid-October. We thought we had been living aboard the boat for several months, but until we sold that last car, we didn't begin to grasp what our new life entailed. Before, as vacation cruisers, we were focused on seeing the sights and finding and enjoying new restaurants and shops. As we looked forward to being in Norfolk tomorrow, we considered our new priorities.

We needed groceries again. We had never realized how much of life centers around food. Since we were no longer able to make a quick stop on the way home to pick up something we needed from the store, we became conscious of how much of our time was spent procuring, storing, and preparing food. As weekend and vacation cruisers, grocery shopping while cruising wasn't really necessary. We had always arrived at the boat laden with enough food to see us through our planned time aboard. If we went grocery shopping, it was because we had a craving for something that we had failed to bring, or we had run out of some specific item. It was something we did for the novelty of it. Now, we were faced with keeping the boat stocked with enough food to last until the next grocery stop, but we didn't know what we would find at the next stop. Sometimes, we weren't even sure where that next stop would be. We did know our way around Norfolk; we knew where to buy a loaf of bread or a can of beans. We knew the general layout of the city, but we realized that we had no idea where to find a real grocery store. And it was not lost on us that Norfolk was our last familiar stop for hundreds of miles.

We needed to do laundry again, too; that had turned out to be a major nuisance. When we lived ashore, we didn't do laundry. Occasionally, one of us would throw something in the washing machine or the dryer, but the chore of laundry day was something we had forgotten. It was never a factor in our weekend or vacation cruising, either. When we had a car to drive from the marina to a self-serve laundry, as we did this summer, it wasn't a big problem. Laundry is probably no one's idea of fun, but it took on a new dimension when it required packing dirty clothes into hand baggage and carrying them to a coin laundry on foot. Then we had to hang around a hot, noisy laundromat while the half-broken machines washed and dried the clothes. After that, we still had to pack them up and carry them back to the boat. It didn't end when we got back to the boat, either.

Play Actor was designed and built for long term cruising. She has far more storage space than most boats her size, but the storage lockers are often oddly shaped, and some are far more readily accessible than others. Each article of clothing had to be folded in a certain way to make it fit in the space allotted. Thought was required in deciding what to put where, and while there was adequate space for our clothes, the space required for a week or two of dirty clothes was something that we hadn't considered before.

We needed to get our mail forwarded to us, as well. It was time to pay some bills and balance the checkbook; in 2012, we do all those things online, but back in 2000, Internet access was limited. It meant finding someone who would allow us to unplug their telephone and plug in our dial-up modem. About all we could do was check email back then. Most financial transactions were done by mail; a few progressive credit cards would accept telephone payments by prior arrangement.

And then, we had a few boat maintenance projects, mostly centered on the engine. *Play Actor* is a sailboat, but during the summer months on the Chesapeake, there's not much wind. There's enough, usually, to enjoy an afternoon of slow sailing, but not enough if you're trying to go somewhere. We had put a lot of hours on the engine recently, and we knew that going south from Norfolk, we would rely on it heavily. Most of the Waterway is too narrow for sailing; there's a reason it's called the Ditch. It was time to change the oil in the engine and the transmission. The cooling system needed to be flushed, and the cooling water pump was due for a rebuild. While it was possible to do all that at anchor, we were worried about having the engine out of commission for several hours at anchor in an unfamiliar place. Suppose one of those snowbirds dragged in a squall and fouled our anchor, leaving us to drift helplessly with our engine disabled?

We concluded that we would book dock space in the Norfolk Municipal Marina at Waterside, right downtown. We had stayed there several times, so it was a comfortable choice. We were beginning to worry a little about how much money we were spending on dockage; it was one of the things that we had not estimated accurately in our budget. Each time we decided to stay in a marina, we rationalized that we had enough money to do what made us feel safe and comfortable.

****

As we entered the Elizabeth River and made our way past the Navy Yard, we remembered our first visit to Norfolk. *Play Actor* had been new to us then, and we had entered the Elizabeth River from the Bay just before dawn. We were dazzled by all the flashing lights on the aids to navigation. The harbor was busy with traffic; our charts were out of date, and we were exhausted and cold. It was mid-November, and winter had come early that year. We finally figured out that while aids to navigation changed often in a place like this, the shoreline was relatively fixed. We hovered off Old Point Comfort trying to get our bearings, and finally set a magnetic course from the Old Point Comfort lighthouse across Hampton Roads to the Elizabeth River entrance, just missing the shallow water off Sewell's Point. We reasoned that those things had not changed since the early exploration of the Bay. As we progressed along the course, the aids to navigation began to make sense. This was before computerized navigation became common for small boats; we still did things the old fashioned way, the way sailors had made landfall for hundreds of years.

By the time the sun was up, we were well into the Elizabeth River, past the bustle of activity at the Navy Yard. We huddled in the cockpit, warming up with cups of ramen noodles and coffee as we watched the shoreline slide by. We were within sight of the marina at Waterside long before their office was open, so we entered slowly and picked out a slip. There were only a few boats in the marina, so we had plenty of room to maneuver. There was a stiff cross-breeze blowing, so we chose a finger pier that would allow us to approach into the wind until the last moment, when we would turn broadside to the wind and coast alongside. We rigged our fenders and dock lines accordingly.

Using the helm and engine controls judiciously, I put the starboard bow neatly against the outermost end of the downwind side of our chosen finger pier, stopping just as Leslie stepped off onto the pier with a mid-ship spring line in her hand. Our plan was that she would secure the line to a cleat at the end of the pier, allowing me to use the engine to move the boat upwind, broadside to the wind and the pier. The spring line and the engine would work against one another, holding us stationary against the pier while we tied the bow and stern lines. This was a familiar maneuver; something we had done many times over the years in various places. The only unfamiliar aspect was the floating finger pier; Norfolk has a tidal range of several feet, unlike the northern part of the Bay, so the finger piers were floats, held in place by pilings. Thus, they could rise and fall with the tide. Having grown up in an area with nine-foot tides, I was accustomed to this, but it was new to Leslie.

She stepped smartly onto the end of the finger pier, which wobbled and sunk an inch or two with her weight. Tired and a bit unsteady on her feet from 24 hours of rolling seas, she was carried forward by her momentum as the pier rolled beneath her feet. She went straight across the narrow pier and into the chilly water on the other side. As she spluttered to the surface, spring line still in hand, a gust of wind piped up, blowing the bow several feet away from the pier. I was now alone on *Play Actor*, my skilled line-handler dog-paddling in her soggy woolen clothes and foul weather gear.

As Leslie, the former competitive swimmer, struggled to make way in her heavy, waterlogged clothing, I realized that the quickest way to get her out of the water was to proceed with our plan. While she was quite at home in the water, hypothermia and her waterlogged clothes were a big worry to me. I knew from my own experience that she probably wouldn't be able to climb out by herself once she managed to swim to a ladder.

"Leslie!" I called.

"Y-y-yes?" she chattered as she was pulled along toward the pier by the line that she still clutched in her left hand.

"While you're there, make that line fast to that cleat right in front of you and hold onto the dock, okay?"

Leslie gave me the disgusted frown that she had heretofore reserved for the children when they misbehaved as she reached for the corner of the dock. I watched her cleat the line, glad that she had practiced doing that so many times, knowing that muscle memory drove her already numb fingers. The spring line was a little longer than we wanted by now, but it would still serve to bring *Play Actor* alongside. I put the transmission in forward and applied a strong burst of power. The movement took the slack out of the line as *Play Actor* surged forward, and then the line stopped her forward motion and she began slipping slowly sideways, into the wind. In under a minute, she was held against the downwind side of the dock by the tension in the line and the thrust of her engine, just as we had planned before Leslie lost her footing. I stepped off onto the dock, quickly tied the bow and stern lines, and helped Leslie drag herself out of the water.

We staggered back aboard, where I shut down the engine and got Leslie below. I lit the cabin heater and helped her get into dry clothes, feeding her hot water until her teeth stopped chattering. I was just starting to think that she was all right when she asked, "Think there's one of those shops that embroiders baseball caps here?"

"What? Why?" I was flummoxed by this, worried now that she was far-gone into a hypothermic delusion of some kind.

"I want one that says, *"Play Actor* – In-water line handler."

I knew then that she was back to normal.

Oenophiles and Snowbirds

Our arrival at Waterside this time was not as exciting as that first time. The winds were calm, and it was midmorning, so there were members of the marina staff to take our dock lines. They wore sweatshirts that said "Human Fender" – not quite like "In-water Line Handler," but still reflecting the entertainment value of watching sailboats maneuver in close quarters. We got *Play Actor* secured and went to the office to check in, where we learned that our stay would be a short one. The Virginia Wine Festival had reserved the entire marina for two days, beginning the next morning.

"Don't worry. There's lots of room in the anchorage right across the river," the manager said.

He was right, but there was a strong cold front in the forecast; we would be anchoring in a spot that's not very well protected from the 25-to-30-knot northwest winds that were expected to accompany the front. There was not much choice, given our list of tasks, so we decided to do laundry at the marina. We could get that done before we had to leave the next morning. Getting ashore with our little rowing dinghy from the anchorage in the sloppy weather to come would be possible, but we wouldn't want to try it laden with our clean clothes; we might get them wet from wind-driven spray. Groceries would survive that better than laundry. We decided to delay our engine maintenance until we could get back into the marina in a couple of days.

Once the laundry was done, we walked the docks, noticing two boats similar in design to *Play Actor*. Aboard one, there was a couple on deck, so we introduced ourselves and inquired about their boat, *China Pearl*, learning that it was a Tayana 37. Bob Perry, the naval architect who designed our boat, also designed the Tayana 37 at about the same time, and they are more similar than different in appearance.

When they learned that we were on *Play Actor,* they told us that their friends just up the dock were on a Tashiba 36 named *China Doll.* The Tashiba 36 is another Perry design. It was the other boat we had noticed, and it's virtually the same design as ours, built in the same shipyard, with just a few minor changes to increase the amount of living space a bit, at the expense of storage. This has been a common occurrence in the evolution of cruising boats over the last few years; not many people actually go cruising, but everybody looks at the bigger living area at the boat shows, and votes with their purchases to favor that design tradeoff. Only later, if ever, do they discover the downside to the choice they made.

As we chatted, the couple from *China Doll* came to visit. Soon, we were touring each others' boats. It was quickly apparent that *China Pearl*, the Tayana 37, was similar in external appearance but quite different in her interior appointments, although she did have a hand-fitted teak interior with the same fine joinery as the Tashiba 36 and *Play Actor*. *China Doll,* the Tashiba 36, was eerily like *Play Actor,* both below deck and above. The most noticeable differences were that the interior space was over a foot wider, yet the exterior width was the same, and she sported a separate shower stall, while our shower was integral to the head. This turned out to have been a major selling point when they bought the boat, giving it an edge in their minds over the older Baba 35s like *Play Actor.*

As we discussed our likes and dislikes, the folks on *China Doll* complained about the lack of storage behind the port and starboard settees; there was little space behind the seat backs, which is where we store all sorts of things. We quickly figured out where the extra one foot plus of interior breadth came from. Their other complaint was that the forward berth was too short for him; he couldn't sleep there, in the master stateroom. That one perplexed us, because their boat was nominally a foot longer than ours, overall. Like the two engineers that we were, he and I took a tape measure to the interiors. Their forward berth was just over six feet long, yet ours, in the shorter boat, was about seven and-a-half feet long. We finally discovered that the extra 18 inches taken from the forward berth had been added to the extra foot in length to gain the space for their stall shower. Tradeoffs like this are a fact of life on boats; that shower didn't look nearly as appealing when Leslie and I discovered that we, both six feet tall, couldn't sleep in the forward berth on the newer boat.

Having spent the afternoon studying each others' boats and cross pollinating all sorts of good ideas for minor improvements, we all decided to go out to dinner at a nice Italian restaurant that we knew from previous visits. We retired to our respective boats to get cleaned up and dressed; dinner out in company was exciting after our hermit-like existence of late. Back on *Play Actor*, Leslie and I took turns showering in our traditional head without a separate shower stall, appreciating it in a way that we had not before. We chatted about our first encounter with other 'full-time' cruisers. The two couples knew one another casually, as they had both spent the summer in the same marina in Connecticut. This was the second southbound journey for both; we were eager to learn what we could from them about the trip. Both had spent last winter in the Bahamas, but only one couple was going back this year. The other folks were planning to spend the winter in Fort Lauderdale, where they were going to do some repairs on their Tayana 37.

We did indeed gain some insights from our dinner companions. The most memorable one came when a harried waiter in the busy restaurant spilled salad dressing on one woman's blouse. When he scurried away to get napkins and soda water to try to clean up the spill, she said, softly, "Damn! This was almost clean when I put it on. I could have worn it several more times." As we continued to adapt to doing laundry over the course of our cruising, we would often recall that remark.

****

The next morning, we moved out of the marina to the anchorage across the river. It takes in several acres of water between Hospital Point and the red channel marker "36," which is the official beginning of the Atlantic Intracoastal Waterway. We anchored the three boats reasonably close together as we planned to get together for cocktails that evening, weather permitting.

As the day wore on, we sat in the cockpit and watched the activity as the marina a few hundred yards away was transformed to a venue for the Wine Show. Boats, mostly good-sized power boats, filled the marina as tents were erected in the adjacent park. While we watched, the warm, sunny day became gloomy; the promised cold front was on the horizon. Late in the afternoon, it arrived, with chilly, gusty winds. We watched carefully to be sure our anchor was holding in the thick mud of the river bottom, and once comfortable, we began to study neighboring boats, particularly the ones upwind. There were no mishaps; everyone stayed put as the chop built from the wind whistling across the width of the river.

At 5:00 p.m., we launched the dinghy and rowed over to *China Pearl* with a plate of cold hors d' oeuvres balanced on Leslie's knees. Besides our new friends, there was an older couple in the cockpit. Introductions disclosed that they were making their 15th trip down the Ditch from Cape Cod on a classic ketch named *Fox Aquila*. Both about 80, they had interesting stories to tell. He was an eighth-generation boat builder from Cape Cod, and had just sold the family business, which had produced innumerable Cape Cod catboats and other wooden-hulled classics during his family's tenure. This was a second marriage for both of them; she had sailed from New England to Europe in the 1950s with her former husband aboard their 35-foot yawl. Her husband died while they were there, "stranding me in Merrie Olde England," she said.

After briefly pondering her plight as a new widow with a yacht in a foreign land, she had decided that the only sensible thing to do was sail home, which she did – alone, across the Atlantic, long before that was common. She had then spent years cruising the East Coast and the islands solo before she met her present husband. After some years of marriage, she had decided that their arrangement seemed secure, so she had found a worthy new owner for her beloved yawl and started cruising with her 'new' husband, the boat builder. They had a small condo in south Florida where they had dock space for their boat, and they enjoyed the seasonal migration that we were eager to experience for the first time.

As the party broke up, we learned that *China Pearl* and *Fox Aquila* were planning a dawn departure the next morning, headed down the Ditch to North Carolina. The folks on *Fox Aquila* knew to the minute what time they needed to leave and how fast they would have to go to arrive at each of the drawbridges along the way in time for their scheduled openings. Their plan was to cross Albemarle Sound, a famously rough, relatively open stretch of water, just as the present cold front was winding down and before the next one hit. "Don't want to cross the sound during a frontal passage; too rough," the lady from *Fox Aquila* remarked.

We spent the next day and night doing odd jobs and reading, waiting for the wind and the Wine Festival to die down. Finally, both things came to pass, and we moved back into Waterside Marina with *China Doll*. We got on with our planned activities, looking forward to cocktail hour aboard *Play Actor* with our new friends. As we sat around *Play Actor's* saloon that night, they teased Leslie unmercifully about her starched, white napkins. "You really are new to this, aren't you?" the woman asked, not in an unkind tone.

"Well, yes," Leslie acknowledged, looking puzzled. They knew well that we were new at this. "Why?"

"You brought these napkins from your house."

"Yes. So what?"

"Most of us use paper napkins, or better yet, paper towels." She saw the dubious look on Leslie's face. "How will you starch them and iron them now?"

"Oh," Leslie said, clearly missing our housekeeper.

Anticipating the Intracoastal Waterway

After our guests left, we were too excited to settle down for the evening. Tomorrow, we would start our trip down the Atlantic Intracoastal Waterway, and my mind was filled with memories of the parts of the Waterway that I knew from my youth. I grew up in Savannah, Georgia, about a mile or two from the Wilmington River, which is the portion of Waterway that was closest to my childhood home. Some of my earliest memories are of watching the traffic on the Wilmington with my father. We would sit on the high bluff on the west side of the river at the little community of Thunderbolt, watching the shrimp boats come and go as they unloaded their catch and took on ice and diesel fuel in preparation for another outing. Tugs would come by with barges laden with pulpwood and other commodities. In the spring and fall, sailboats would pass as they followed the sun north or south. "Rich Yankees," my father would remark, with no hint of envy.

My father was an avid fisherman, and by the time I was four, he took me with him on his jaunts. He owned a series of small boats, and we fished the waters along the Waterway from the Carolinas down into Florida until I was in college, so I knew what to expect from the Waterway, but it would all be new to Leslie. Early in our marriage, I had taken her to Thunderbolt, but most of the shrimp boats had moved elsewhere, and the bluff had been taken over by marinas and waterfront restaurants. I was looking forward to introducing her to some of the unspoiled wilderness and the quaint, colonial-era towns that bordered the Ditch on some of its less populated stretches.

Much of the Waterway comprises natural estuaries behind sandy barrier islands that make up the East Coast from Norfolk, Virginia, south to Key West, Florida. Every so often, there are inlets through the barrier islands. Some are large and deep, allowing ships to reach the deepwater ports along the East Coast, but many are shallow and treacherous, providing access to the sea only for tiny local fishing boats. When a major storm rakes the coast, new inlets open up and old ones disappear as the sands of the barrier islands shift at the whim of Mother Nature. The ephemeral nature of most of the barrier islands is the reason that those who know the coast have little interest in owning beachfront property. In the stretches where the natural channels fail to connect with one another or are too shallow for navigation, the U.S. Army Corps of Engineers has built canals and dredged the natural channels to provide a protected, inland route of sufficient depth and breadth to allow commercial traffic, as well as providing a major recreational resource.

Sometimes known as the nation's first highway, the Waterway and the towns along it have been important to commerce since colonial days. U.S. Highway 1 and its derivatives, including the newest, Interstate 95, carry a lot of freight up and down the East Coast, but in our country's early history, ships were the preferred means of moving cargo, being both faster and less expensive than land transportation. In the early days, those places with deep water access became hubs of commerce, and some remain so today. Others have literally disappeared, having fallen to competition from air, rail, and trucks. The inland estuaries provided distribution from the seaports to the centers of agriculture, mining, and manufacturing.

Efforts to connect and improve the natural Waterways to support waterborne commerce began early in our history. The Dismal Swamp Canal, which provides a protected, all-weather, inland route from the Chesapeake Bay to Albemarle Sound in North Carolina, is the oldest continually operating man-made canal in the U.S. George Washington surveyed the route and proposed a canal in the 1760s, well before the revolution. It was clear even then that the ability to move goods from the Carolina plantations to the great natural seaport at Norfolk without venturing into the treacherous, shoaling waters along the North Carolina coast would be of strategic economic importance.

The canal opened in 1805. Although Washington didn't live to see it, he was one of the original shareholders in the company that owned the canal. In the early years of the 19th century, the British Navy still harassed coastal shipping in North America, which provided an additional impetus to our forefathers to develop the inland waterways as a means of transportation and distribution. The U.S. Army Corps of Engineers produced an interesting history of the inland waterways in 1983. It's available as a free PDF download; the title is "History of the Waterways of the Atlantic Coast of the United States."

Besides its commercial importance, the Intracoastal Waterway provides a protected route for recreational vessels. An ocean-going sailboat like our *Play Actor* could certainly make the trip offshore between the major natural harbors along the East Coast, but sailing vessels are at the mercy of the prevailing winds and ocean currents. The Gulf Stream is a major consideration for shipping along the East Coast, especially in those areas where the Stream is close to shore and shoal waters extend far out to sea.

Cape Hatteras and Cape Fear along the North Carolina coast are two such places, and the weather systems that move across the North American continent make their already treacherous waters prone to frequent and somewhat unpredictable storms. The sea off Hatteras has long been known as 'the graveyard of ships' because of these factors. A safe southbound passage around the capes under sail requires venturing well over a hundred miles offshore, unless the weather is settled and the vessel is prepared to use an auxiliary engine to supplement the unpredictable winds. A northbound passage through the same waters is quite different, as the Gulf Stream provides a favorable current of several knots to northbound vessels.

These phenomena are the reason that the typical trade routes in the days of sail had southbound ships leaving from New England to ride the prevailing winds roughly six hundred miles southeast to Bermuda. From Bermuda, they would catch the easterly trade winds for a relatively easy trip south of about a thousand miles to the eastern Caribbean. From the Caribbean, the prevailing winds and currents are favorable for sailing to the southeast coast of North America, perhaps to Savannah or Charleston. Going north from there, it is safe to stay reasonably close to shore until Cape Fear, providing access to a number of good deep water inlets. Southport, Wilmington, and Beaufort are all safe inlets. Northbound sailing vessels normally stood well offshore from Cape Fear north to the Chesapeake Bay entrance. From Norfolk to New England was a relatively easy near-coastal route. All this had a profound impact on the development of commerce in the early days of our country. It is not an accident that the major cities of the East Coast have good deep-water inlets and harbors; it's why they are where they are. A safe, protected inland waterway was of major commercial significance, as it allowed smaller vessels to move goods from north to south by a much more direct route.

Although we could have taken *Play Actor* south by the traditional, offshore route, our choice was to take the inland route, or the "Ditch," as it is often called. We wanted to see the scenery and explore the towns along the way, planning to move south just fast enough to stay ahead of winter weather, following the fall foliage as it crept south along with the cold weather. An additional attraction of the Ditch is that it's possible to do the 1,000-mile trip from Norfolk, Virginia, to south Florida a day at a time, stopping to rest anywhere that fancy dictates. This is of no small importance for a two-person crew; the offshore route requires that someone sail the boat 24 hours a day, seven days a week. There are no 'rest areas' at sea, but there are numerous places to stop along the Waterway.

Part of the Snowbird Flock – Dismal Swamp Canal

We timed our departure from Waterside so we would reach the first drawbridge during the window of time when it would open for us. Drawbridges would be more of a factor in our travels than we had realized; at 57 feet, our mast was too tall to fit under many of the bridges that span the Waterway. Most of the newer bridges, especially on heavily travelled roads, have 65 feet of clearance, which will accommodate most cruising boats that use the Waterway, but many of the older bridges, including railroad bridges, are too low for us. They were built when the roads weren't as heavily travelled and the expense of tall bridges wasn't warranted.

Motorists and dirt-dwellers, as we are learning to call our shore-bound brethren, find the disruption to traffic from drawbridges to be annoying. Why, they wonder, should they have to wait for slow-moving boats? Historically, the traffic on the water has the right-of-way; it was there first, and it is often involved in federally protected, interstate commerce, so the state and local authorities don't have a free hand in managing the traffic tradeoffs. Unless bridges open on request for traffic on the water, opening schedules must be approved by the federal authorities, ensuring some balancing of interests.

We were excited to be exploring new waters. The people on *China Doll* were stuck in Norfolk for a few more days waiting for a shipment of boat parts to arrive. We hoped that they would catch up with us farther south; we enjoyed their company. We accomplished most of our missions in Norfolk, although there was a problem with our mail. The people who ran the service that we used had been unable to get into their office for several days as a result of some natural disaster, so we made arrangements with them to have our mail sent to general delivery in Elizabeth City, North Carolina, instead of Norfolk. We had one credit card bill that was due in the meantime, but we made a payment by telephone, so we were comfortable with the notion that we would be out of touch for a couple of days.

As we got closer to that first drawbridge, we merged with a steady stream of southbound sailboats. There were a few motor yachts and a small number of commercial vessels, mostly harbor tugs with a barge or two laden with some commodity. All of us were converging on the span of that bridge, doing our best to stay clear of one another as the wind and current pushed our boats around in an unpredictable manner. The brand-new skippers among us were quickly apparent as their stress levels built; there was arm waving, yelling, and occasional cursing as the crowd of boats drifted inexorably closer together and closer to the bridge.

Sailboats under power are notoriously hard to control in close quarters and at low speeds. They depend on the flow of water against the underwater surfaces for directional stability and control, much as airplanes depend on the flow of air over wings and control surfaces. When an airplane ceases to move fast enough, it falls from the sky; when a sailboat ceases to move fast enough, it drifts at the mercy of the wind and water currents, but each sailboat drifts differently, so some drift uncomfortably close to others.

Before any of the waiting boats actually hit one another, we heard the siren from the bridge, signaling that it was about to open. We watched as the cross-arms came down, closing the bridge approaches to land traffic, and new waves of stress passed through the crowd of waiting boats as some surged forward, driven by the compulsion to be "first." We waited patiently, merged with the less eager traffic, and ended up passing through the open span of the bridge in the middle of the pack.

As the tightly clustered boats began to spread out on the downstream side of the bridge, Leslie and I talked about the irony of the behavior we've just witnessed. We had contemplated this cruising life as an escape from the rat-race for a long time, and surely, most of those other folks had, as well. Yet, a substantial number of them brought the rat-race mentality with them, as evidenced by their need to defend their territorial patch of water and their compulsion to get ahead of the other boats.

We chuckled at the thought of how frustrating this cruising life would be for them; we had already discovered how elusive and illusory our control over what happened with the boat really was. We had years to learn that the rhythms of this life on the water were established by the rhythms of nature, not by clocks and calendars. We wondered if some of those folks would be so compelled to get ahead of the boat in front that they would miss the scenery that we all dreamed of seeing. Most of the people who set out to do what we were doing professed to believe that the journey was at least as important as the destination, but the behavior of many belied that cliché.

And then there were a few who heard a different drummer. One medium-sized powerboat was staying just a few feet behind a tug, which was pulling a barge-load of sand as we approached the bridge. We saw the names on the transoms as they passed us, and we heard the skipper of the power boat calling the tug on the VHF radio. The names have been changed to protect the foolish. "Tug *Night Hawk, Night Hawk, Night Hawk,* this is the motor yacht *Dreamboat* on your stern. Over." There was no response from the tug, and the call was repeated, with a tone of impatience. This time the captain of the tug responded, and having spent years among folks like him, I formed a clear mental image of him shifting his plug of chewing tobacco to the side of his mouth before he keyed the microphone.

"This here's the *Night Hawk.* Yew that little white cabin cruiser doggin' me?"

"*Night Hawk,* this is the motor yacht *Dreamboat* on your stern. Over."

"G' mornin', Captain. This the *Night Hawk.* Whut kin I do fer ye?"

"*Night Hawk,* is this what they call the Intracoastal Waterway? Over."

"It shore is, Captain! Yew done found it! Congratulations to ye!"

"Thank you very much, *Night Hawk.* I'm bound for Florida. Can I just follow you? Over."

"Well, you shore can, I reckon, but I ain't a goin' to no Florida. I'm a turnin' off jus' befo' the nex' bridge. Gonna drop this here barge 'n' pick up a empty one to take back up to the Spit. Yew welcome to foller me, though, if'n tha's what yew wantin' to do."

Dreamboat was silent.

There was less drama as we approached the next drawbridge, just a few minutes ahead. The gating function of the last bridge had forced the traffic into a more orderly pattern, and the next bridge was opened on a schedule coordinated with the last one. As the boats ahead of us passed through the bridge, we listened to more chatter on the VHF radio. We recognized that there were clusters of boats -- people who knew one another and were sticking together. The VHF radio was like a party-line telephone; it provided endless opportunities for amusing eavesdropping. There were several conversations about the choice of route across the Virginia-North Carolina border. Most people were planning to take the "Virginia cut" route, which is the main channel of the Waterway and would have them in Coinjock, North Carolina, for the evening. "It's faster," we heard. "Yeah. Safer, too. I heard about a guy who hit a log in the Dismal Swamp. Had to be towed. Thousands of dollars in damage," another person remarked. "It's really shallow; easy to get stuck. They should close it."

We were planning to take the Dismal Swamp Canal; it's a not-to-be-missed piece of living history. We were intrigued by the misinformation on the rumor mill; before we made our decision as to route, I called the Corps of Engineers office in Norfolk and talked with one of the project managers who filled me in on the latest information on the Dismal Swamp Canal. It had been cleared and dredged in a few places in the last few months, and it had a controlling (minimum) depth of six feet. That made us a little nervous, as our draft is just a few inches less than six feet, leaving little margin for error. The man I spoke with assured me that most of it was deeper, and that while we might occasionally touch the bottom, the bottom was covered with several feet of soft silt and would cause us no problems. "Besides," he finished, "it's easily the most beautiful part on the ICW. Don't miss it."

When we turned off into Deep Creek, the approach to the Dismal Swamp Canal, from the upper reach of the Elizabeth River, we left the crowd behind. About two miles up Deep Creek, we came to the Deep Creek lock, the entrance to the Dismal Swamp Canal, at about 10 o'clock. The next scheduled opening of the lock was at 11, so we dropped our anchor and had coffee in the cockpit, enjoying the relative solitude after our time in Norfolk. By 11 o'clock, a few more boats appeared, and we all passed through the lock together, visiting with the friendly lock keeper while the water surged into the chamber, lifting us about nine feet to the level of the water in the swamp.

Soon, we were motoring down the canal, indeed a beautiful, almost surreal place. Obviously man-made, the canal is straight and narrow; it's probably 75 feet from bank to bank, but it seems narrower, and the lush vegetation on both sides hangs out over the water. Our mast brushed tree limbs every so often, accumulating clumps of Spanish moss as we watched for the otters and beavers playing along the banks. Sometimes we could feel our keel dragging through the soft mud of the canal bottom, and once in a while there was a solid thump as we passed over a log on the bottom, but, as the man from the Corps of Engineers promised, we had no problems. By about three in the afternoon, we arrived at the Dismal Swamp Canal Welcome Center, right on the Virginia-North Carolina state line. The center serves motorists on Highway 17 as well as boat traffic on the canal; there's a nice dock, completely filled by earlier arrivals when we pulled in sight that afternoon.

As we approached the dock, some folks on a trawler yacht tied to the dock waved us alongside, encouraging us to tie up to their boat for the night. We took advantage of their offer and learned that they were former sailors. They had decided that if they were only going to cruise the Waterway, a powerboat with all its amenities made more sense than a sailboat. We learned that the boats alongside the dock had all come through the 8:30 a.m. lock from Deep Creek. By early evening, several more boats had arrived, having come through the 1:30 and 3:30 lock openings, and the boats were rafted three abreast along the dock.

Given the number of boats tied together in close proximity, the night was still and quiet; everyone was pleasantly tired and looking forward to an early departure in the morning. We all planned to make the 8:30 lock at South Mills the next morning; the lock was a little over an hour's travel farther south. That would put us in Elizabeth City, North Carolina, sometime the next afternoon.

Dismal Swamp Canal to Elizabeth City, N.C.

We were up at sunrise, as were our neighbors. We all planned to leave at about seven to make the 8:30 lock at the south end of the Dismal Swamp Canal, and after a quick breakfast, we began sorting out the boats. With all the later arrivals yesterday, we were packed three deep against the dock. Everyone pitched in to help the outer rank of boats get free, and soon it was our turn to join the parade. We motored south, admiring the fall colors in some of the trees as we spotted the occasional granite mile-markers on the bank, relics of the canal's early days.

At about 7:30, we had the South Mills lock in sight. Just a few hundred yards from the lock, there is a draw bridge. This mirrors the situation at the north end of the canal. The lock keepers double as bridge tenders, and once they shepherd the boats through the first barrier, they hop into a car and drive to the next one. As we approached the bridge, we saw that a few boats had actually spent the night tied to the bridge abutments. They apparently decided that the dock at the Welcome Center was too crowded and passed it by yesterday afternoon.

All but one of the boats tied to the abutment cast off their lines and joined the crowd, hovering near the bridge, waiting for the lock keeper to show up. The one boat that remained tied to the abutment was a beautiful new ketch about 45 feet in length. The couple aboard explained to folks on several nearby boats that they would wait for the crowd to pass and go through the bridge last, as they were facing the wrong direction and would need plenty of space to turn around in the narrow canal. It did appear that their boat was almost as long as the distance between the bridge abutments, so we didn't blame them for worrying a bit.

At 8:15, a pickup truck pulled to a stop outside the bridge tender's hut, and the lock keeper climbed from the truck and unlocked the hut housing the controls for the bridge. In a minute or two, he announced on the VHF radio that he would be raising the bridge and that all the boats should pass through and wait for him to close the bridge and drive down to the lock. A minute later, the bells began ringing and the arms came down across the road. The draw span went up, and we joined the parade of boats passing through. As the last boat entered the span, the big ketch that had been facing the wrong way pulled away from the abutment with a roar of the diesel and a cloud of black smoke as the skipper pushed the throttle all the way open, suddenly in an obvious hurry. He turned the helm sharply to the port and the boat responded more quickly than I would have expected.

He was watching the stern to be sure it cleared the abutment behind him as he turned sharply to the left. By now, the boat was at a right angle to the channel with the bow pointed at the opposite bridge abutment as the heavy vessel accelerated. Satisfied that his stern would swing clear, he turned and looked toward the bow. We were close enough to see the fleeting look of terror cross his features. We heard the engine race as he jerked the transmission through neutral and into reverse without throttling back, trying in vain to stop the boat. The water boiled under the stern of the boat as the propeller fought for purchase. His wife stood on the bow, facing backward, watching him. We winced as he screamed, "Fend off, dammit! Now, Helen! Wake up, stupid!"

She shrugged, confusion evident as she tried to understand what he wanted her to do. The bow of the boat smashed into the abutment with a resounding crash, and his wife was thrown to the deck by the impact. The gleaming stainless steel of the bow rail was now shaped like a pretzel, and the bow was a wreck of shattered fiberglass. "Dammit! I told you to fend off," the man screamed as his wife struggled to regain her feet.

"Look out!" She yelled at her apoplectic husband, raising an arm to point helplessly behind them, just as the boat, now accelerating rapidly in reverse, crashed stern-first into the other abutment. She was holding on this time, having seen it coming, but he wasn't. After falling backward against the now-crumpled stern rail, he got back to his feet. This time, he remembered the throttle before he shifted into forward. In the panic of the moment, he again opened the throttle all the way, and the boat obediently surged forward. He continued to smash the boat first into one wall, and then into the other, until he finally had it angled into the opening of the draw. By then, he was far over to one side of the opening, and he snagged the boat's rigging on the end of the draw bridge, some 35 to 40 feet in the air. The rigging gave way, but not before the boat smashed into the side of the opening, spun by the pull of the rigging wire before the wire snapped. The bridge tender scrambled down to the abutment and took a stern line from them, helping them pull the wrecked vessel back to the spot where they had been tied up a few minutes before.

The bridge closed, dropping the curtain on the morning's drama, and the rest of us watched as the lock keeper drove to the lock. Once he reached the controls, the gate swung open and we all moved soberly into the chamber, tying off to the sides. As the early entrants waited for the later ones to secure themselves for the locking, passengers stepped off their boats and began to circulate, chatting. The word spread that the ketch which had the problem was brand new; she had been the retirement dream of the man who had effectively demolished her before our eyes. He and his wife had no boating experience, and their trip south from New England had been plagued by mishaps, although none of this magnitude. The lock keeper told us quietly that the couple had told him they were going to take the boat to Norfolk and sell it. We were all saddened to have witnessed such a nightmarish ending to their dream.

Once through the South Mills lock, we had a short stretch of canal that took us to the main course of the Pasquotank River. The misty beauty of the Pasquotank as it wound through virgin cypress swamp has haunted us ever since. It had a timeless, other-worldly quality; it would have been no surprise to round the next bend and find dinosaurs eating some prehistoric fish, or an encampment of early humans going about their daily business. As we wound our way downstream, the river broadened and lost its ethereal air, but it was still quite beautiful.

During the several hours between the South Mills lock and the draw bridge at the upstream side of Elizabeth City, the boats which had come out of the lock together had spread out over several miles, some stopping to anchor for lunch in some of the inviting oxbows, others opting to stay for a night or two in this pristine wilderness. It was hard to believe that we were only a little over an hour by car from the bustle of Norfolk.

Leslie and I were both sorry to have witnessed the debacle involving the boat at the drawbridge; we knew how eager we had been to undertake our own adventure. While we had experienced a few setbacks, surprises, and disappointments, we could only imagine what that couple must be feeling. We were thankful that we had given ourselves the years of weekend experience before we made the leap. Most of our skills were acquired so gradually that we can't remember learning them, and trying to imagine what it would be like to take off and do this with no background seemed inconceivable to us. We understood that many people did exactly that, and many of those eventually developed sufficient skills to see them through. A fair number of people, however, didn't, and we had already heard that some marriages didn't survive the cruising experience, either. We wondered what would become of the couple on the ketch back in South Mills.

Our period of introspection was short-lived, though. Soon we were through the next drawbridge, which opened on request except during the morning and evening rush hours. We idled slowly past the seawall along the park in downtown Elizabeth City, studying the docking facilities. There was a row of pilings 30 to 50 feet out from the seawall, spaced just far enough apart to allow a boat to squeeze between them. Docking along the seawall was free, compliments of the town. There were a few boats there already, bows tied to the seawall, with stern lines and spring lines to the pilings. We found a berth that had a short finger pier and pulled in, securing *Play Actor* with no difficulty, glad of the finger pier as our bowsprit would have otherwise been a serious obstacle to going ashore. As it was, the finger pier came out just far enough so that we could make it from the boat to the pier with a stretch of our legs.

As we got ourselves settled, an elderly man in a golf cart pulled up in front of the boat and climbed out. "Good afternoon, folks. I'm Fred Fearing, one of the original 'Rose Buddies,' and I want to welcome you to my home town." With a gracious flourish, he presented Leslie with a single red rose, matching the one painted on the water tower which we could see in the distance. "A beautiful flower for a beautiful lady," he said.

We spent a few minutes visiting with Fred before another boat came along. As I excused myself to go and help the new arrival with their dock lines, Fred said, "Now don't forget, there'll be complimentary wine and cheese right over yonder at 5:00 o'clock sharp to welcome all you folks on boats to Elizabeth City. Y'all come! We thank you for stopping to visit." He climbed into the golf cart and drove down a few yards to the next boat.

Coping with Equipment Failure in a Strange Place

There were over 30 boats tied up to the seawall by the time the wine and cheese party started, and Leslie and I both fell back on old habits, splitting up to work the crowd. We both enjoyed ourselves, and we met some interesting people. The gathering broke up after about an hour and a half, and we returned to *Play Actor* for a light dinner during which we compared notes on the people we had met. We were surprised at how many couples were younger; several were in their 30s and 40s and were out for a year or two of adventure, expecting to return to the working world when they had to. As we had expected, there were a number of couples of normal retirement age. We didn't fit either group; Leslie was at the upper end of the young crowd, and I was a good bit younger than the retired people. The dynamics of the crowd were interesting; people from similar backgrounds quickly found one another, and most conversations centered around former lives, rather than expectations for their cruising adventures. That seemed reasonable enough, as most of the crowd had spent no more than a few weeks aboard their boats.

When we listened to the weather the next morning, we learned that we were likely to spend the next several days in Elizabeth City. That next cold front would be upon us in a few hours, with howling northerly winds. Had we chosen to run for it, we would have been caught in the open on Albemarle Sound when the leading edge of the front hit. The sound is wide and shallow, and we had read and heard that it could get very rough very quickly, so we dawdled over breakfast and coffee. We figured we would need to pace ourselves, or we would run out of things to see and do in Elizabeth City before lunch time – it's an attractive town, but definitely on the small side.

As Leslie was cleaning up after breakfast, I went up on deck to check our mooring lines. Where we were sitting would be relatively exposed, and the wide bend in the river where Elizabeth City is situated would allow a substantial chop to build as the wind-driven waves hit the seawall where we were tied. We expected that our ride might become uncomfortable, and I was worried that the dock lines would chafe from the motion of the boat. As I surveyed our situation, I noticed that the depth sounder wasn't working; I finished adjusting the lines and went below.

Play Actor had a typical complement of instruments for a boat her age; they had been state of the art when she was originally commissioned, 20 years before. They weren't as small and elegant as the current generation of sailboat instruments, but they delivered the same information: water depth, wind speed, wind direction in degrees off the bow of the boat, and speed through the water. There was a display at the helm and a duplicate display below at the nav station. I checked the instruments at the nav station and discovered that the depth reading wasn't available there, either. Clicking through the other functions, I found erratic readings for wind speed, as well. I forgot about my worries as to how we would amuse ourselves; I had a new boat project.

This wasn't the first problem we had experienced with these instruments; we had owned the boat for over 12 years already at that time. I had the service manuals, and within an hour, I had isolated the problem to one circuit board. If the board was bad, we not only would be missing depth and wind speed information; we wouldn't have our speed through the water, either. I removed and examined the offending circuit board, seeing nothing obviously amiss. I cleaned the connections and put it back, but that didn't solve the problem. Repairing the board itself outside of a laboratory wasn't realistic; normal service procedure would be to replace the board. Unfortunately, the instruments had been manufactured in the U.S., back when we used to actually build things instead of just designing them for offshore manufacture. The company was no longer in business, and replacement parts weren't available.

Reluctantly, we accepted that we needed new instruments. It was hard to be too upset about that; these had worked for 20 years. We swallowed hard at the prospect of spending $5,000, though. We were already struggling with the idea that, after years of working hard and saving our money, we were spending our savings. After watching our net worth grow for all those years, we were seeing it begin to decline. Our plan had been to live on the income from our savings, most of which were invested in conservative mutual funds. We had spent four months living as if we were on an extended vacation, ignoring the fact that we were no longer in the upper income bracket. It had been easy to rationalize one more expensive meal out, or one more night in a marina. $5,000 dollars was a significant percentage of our planned annual budget; the prospect of such a large, unexpected expenditure was a shock.

We had spent a lot of money on the boat in the last couple of years that we worked, bringing her up to first-rate condition in anticipation of long-term cruising. We had focused on the things that affected her seaworthiness first and cosmetics second. By the time we finished, we had spent as much as she was worth, but that was a conscious choice; we liked the design, and new boats weren't being built to the same standards. We had considered replacing her with a newer boat, and decided to refurbish her instead. When we did that, we were paying for the work easily out of current income. This decision about the instruments was different. The prospect of writing a check for $5,000 back when we were both working wouldn't have been so daunting, but we could see a small but direct relationship between the purchase of new instruments and the end of our liquidity.

And then there was the problem of actually installing new instruments. Our conditioned response to problems like this had always been to get the boat back to her home port, where we could deal with the trouble at our leisure. For as long as we had owned big sailboats, we had kept them near major working boat yards where this sort of work was easily handled. We remembered our reaction to the leaking muffler a few weeks earlier; that was exactly how we had handled it. We had, effectively, gone 'home' to a familiar, comfortable place, where it was easy to find parts and accomplish the repair.

The reality of our chosen new life confronted us squarely: 'home' was wherever we found ourselves. Home was no longer a fixed place to which we could run for succor when things didn't suit us. We maintained a mailing address in Florida because of the state's tax laws, but Florida was far away, and we had no physical 'home' there in any case. Conceptually, we had understood that we would need to repair the boat during the course of our travels, but we had not been forced to consider what that involved until the instruments quit working.

People we met at the wine and cheese party began to drop by as the morning wore on, distracting us a bit. One couple, from St. Michael's, Maryland, suggested lunch in a bakery and sandwich shop that they knew from a previous visit. We had enjoyed chatting with them last night; we had a lot in common with them, including many of the places we had lived during our period as corporate nomads. They were older, retired for a few years, but they had taken a year off to cruise the Waterway about 15 years previously, and were experienced sailors, revisiting the places they had enjoyed in their earlier travels. Their reaction to our problem with the instruments was the same as ours. Navigation instruments were essential.

As we walked back through town after lunch, the four of us ran into another couple who had just arrived that morning. They were old friends of our new acquaintances and were closer to us in age. They had been cruising part-time for many years, spending their time off the boat by touring the U.S. with a 35-foot travel trailer. They were on their way to the post office to get their mail, so we accompanied them, hoping that ours would be there as well. Their views on the instruments were no different; we had to have them. We got our mail, and the six of us went back to our boats, talking about where we might do the instrument replacement job.

I grew up working on boats, and my undergraduate degree is in electrical engineering; I spent much of my career in the high-tech world. Actually doing the work of removing the old instruments and putting in new ones was not a worrisome prospect for me. The problem was twofold. First, we needed to acquire the instruments, and second, we needed to haul the boat out of the water, as some of the work would involve installing transducers that actually penetrated the hull below the waterline. Our friends thought that the two closest places that would accommodate both requirements were Norfolk, two days behind us, or Beaufort, North Carolina, a few days ahead of us. We spent the rest of the afternoon pondering our options.

By dinnertime, the promised cold front had materialized, and we had a bouncy evening as the wind howled and the choppy waves jerked at our dock lines. Periodically, one of us checked the lines for chafe. Breaking a dock line under these conditions would cause the boat to grind against the concrete seawall a few feet in front of us. Kept awake by the weather, we lit the diesel heater and sat in the saloon, reading and sharing our thoughts on our dilemma.

We didn't want to go back to Norfolk; it was getting cold. Beaufort was at least in the right direction, and it had the reputation of being a yachting center with several full service yards where we could do the work. The prospect of navigating 150 miles of the notoriously shallow Waterway without a depth sounder was daunting. I remembered my childhood fishing trips with my father; one of my early jobs was to cast the sounding lead.

For thousands of years, mariners relied on a length of line with a heavy weight on the end to find the depth of the water under their keel. The line was marked in a variety of ways, and the person with the lead-line called out the soundings to the person piloting the boat; one of my favorite writers took his pen name from his days calling out soundings on the Mississippi river, where the depth was often, "By the mark, twain," the traditional call for two fathoms. We carried the lead-line from my father's last boat aboard *Play Actor*, but the notion of standing on the bow tossing the sounding lead and retrieving it for several days wasn't appealing.

The reminiscence did serve to clear our thoughts, though. We realized that the essential part of the instrument package was the depth sounder. Speed through the water was useful but not essential for our purposes; the real utility of speed data historically was that it allowed the navigator to compute the distance traveled from the last known location. Distance traveled from your last known location and the direction of travel from a compass allowed you to estimate your current position. In the Ditch, we could look at the shoreline; we didn't have to estimate our position, and besides, we had GPS. GPS gave us our exact position, accurate to within a few feet, as well as giving us our speed over the ground, which, for navigating, was more useful than speed through the water.

Wind speed and direction, the other information from a typical sailboat instrument system, were of little practical use, except perhaps to racers. You had too much wind for your sails, the right amount, or not enough. In the first case, you reduced the amount of sail; in the second, you enjoyed the trip, and in the last case, you added more sail. As for wind direction, there was an old fashioned weather vane at the top of our mast. We finally realized that all we really *needed* was a depth sounder.

We pulled out the dog-eared catalog from our favorite marine supply house and discovered that basic depth sounders could be had for as little as $100. The parameters of our problem changed; the question became, "How quickly can we get one of those, here in Elizabeth City?" We walked about a half a mile to the nearest marina, which mainly catered to small local boats. They had a $100 depth sounder in stock, which we promptly purchased. Feeling significantly better about life, we went back to *Play Actor* and installed our new instrument. Rather than have the boat hauled out of the water, which was still a problem – *Play Actor* tips the scales at almost 30,000 pounds – we decided to install the transducer inside the hull rather than cutting a hole through the bottom.

I had some experience with that sort of installation in the early days of electronic depth sounders, and I knew it could work. The instructions advised that the transducer could be glued to the inside of the hull with epoxy. As this would be permanent, it was further recommended that the transducer be tested by holding it in place after smearing grease over the surface to eliminate any voids and air bubbles. We tested it as advised, and it worked beautifully. Still, I wasn't ready to glue it in with epoxy. If we wanted to move it for some reason, we would most likely destroy the transducer while breaking it free. I opted to glue it in place with silicone sealant, which also seemed to work well.

Feeling just a little pride at how we had solved our problem, we set about enjoying our forced stay in Elizabeth City. We found a surprising number of things to amuse ourselves, including an interesting little historical museum (since replaced by a much finer one, we hear) on the outskirts of town. There were a couple of good used book stores, where we were able to stock our bookshelves, and there were endless opportunities to socialize with our fellow travelers, who were also growing restless as the foul weather kept us pinned to the seawall. After several days of this, we got a positive forecast for a few days. Everybody made last minute runs to the small local grocery stores, jugged fuel from the corner gas station, and generally got ready to go. We noticed that our new depth sounder was no longer working.

We frantically cut the transducer free of the silicone that held it against the inside of the bottom. Dangling it from its cable, I lowered it carefully into the water beside the boat as Leslie watched the display. It worked once the transducer was below the surface. I theorized that I must have trapped air bubbles in the silicone when I glued it in place, so I cleaned the contact surfaces thoroughly and tried gluing it in with more silicone. It worked well; we relaxed again. We went to bed early that night, planning a dawn departure along with all our eager compatriots.

Albemarle Sound and a Leaky Coolant Pump

The next day dawned as promised by NOAA, something that we had learned not to take for granted. We joined the crowd of boats dropping dock lines and backing out into the Pasquotank River, bound for the other side of Albemarle Sound. Once we were a few hundred yards from the bend in the river where the town was, the river broadened dramatically, and we found a favorable sailing breeze. Almost everyone raised sails, and the boats began to spread out along the route. Most of us kept our engines on as well to ensure that we made good speed, at least to the open water of Albemarle Sound. The first good anchorage on the other side of the sound was over 50 miles away, with one drawbridge to slow us down, and the days were getting short. Distances on the Waterway are measured in statute miles rather than the slightly longer nautical miles to which we are more accustomed, but even so, we felt the need to push ourselves in order to avoid having to anchor in a strange place in the dark.

By the time we reached the sound, we had solid 15-knot wind on the port beam, giving us a rollicking ride across the sound, which was still fairly rough from the high winds of the previous several days. As we reached the dogleg channel at the entrance to the Alligator River on the south side of the sound, we started the engine to help negotiate the narrow bends of the entrance. Once in the relative protection of the river, the wind began to drop, and we motor-sailed the rest of the way to our chosen anchorage. We followed the broad part of the river south until it made a sharp, 90-degree bend to the east, where it also narrowed dramatically, providing good all-around protection with plenty of room to anchor well to the north of the channel.

Pleased that our new depth sounder was working so well, we enjoyed sundowners in the cockpit. It was cool but not unpleasant; there was no wind to chill us as the sun's warmth faded. We were tired; we made a quick dinner and read for a while, enjoying the feeling that we were finally settling in to our new life. At about nine o'clock that evening, we heard the distant rumble of a powerful diesel growing closer by the minute. Soon, a strong spotlight swept across *Play Actor,* flashing through the glass port lights into the cabin. I stepped up into the cockpit to make sure that we were safely out of the way, watching for a few minutes as a tug with several heavily laden barges passed a few hundred yards to the south of us. As I got ready to go back below, I glanced at the depth sounder and noticed that it wasn't working.

Frustrated now, ready for bed but knowing that I wouldn't be able to sleep, I cut the transducer free of the silicone again and lowered it over the side. It worked perfectly. Thinking for a few minutes, I reasoned that as the silicone cured, it must have changed density so that it attenuated the ultrasonic pulses from the transducer. The logic was seductively clear. I understood what was going on, but I didn't want to devise a permanent solution this late in the evening, and we wanted to move on in the morning. We talked it over and came up with an interim solution. We fastened the transducer to the end of our eight-foot aluminum boathook pole with lots of duct tape and lashed the pole vertically to one of the lifeline stanchions. This positioned the transducer about a foot below the surface of the water and on the outside of the starboard side of *Play Actor's* hull. It looked strange, and it would certainly create drag as the boat moved through the water, probably slowing us down incrementally, but it would work until we reached a spot where we wanted to spend a little time. Then I could devise a better way to fasten the transducer to the inside of the hull.

We took a look at the charts and realized that we could plan a short day tomorrow, stopping for diesel fuel in Belhaven, North Carolina, and anchoring there in mid-afternoon, giving us time to make a permanent repair to the troublesome depth sounder. As we climbed under the covers, we noticed the unearthly quiet as we dropped off to sleep; we were truly in the middle of nowhere.

The next day, we bought diesel fuel and anchored in Pungo Creek, just south of Belhaven. We were by ourselves, wondering where all the other boats went. I ground the inner surface of the hull completely flat with a big angle grinder, finishing the surface to a matte texture where we had been trying to fasten the depth transducer. Holding the transducer gently against the now smooth surface produced good readings of depth, so I secured it with a thin bead of silicone around the outer edge, careful to press it down firmly to make a mechanical connection between the two surfaces, with no attenuating layer of silicone in between.

****

As we pulled out of Pungo Creek the next morning, we joined the parade of boats again. We wondered where they had been, but it didn't occur to us to call anyone on the radio to ask. As we crossed Pamlico Sound and entered the Neuse River, we did turn on the radio to eavesdrop. We learned that the crowd was planning to anchor in Adams Creek that night. We studied the chart and decided that Adams Creek would be crowded; we decided to stop a couple of miles before that, turning off into the South River instead. We learned from the people we met in Elizabeth City that most of them were using an inexpensive guide to anchorages on the Waterway, rather than consulting their navigation charts and picking anchorages on their own. There was a herd mentality at work among a lot of our fellow cruisers; we wondered where the adventure was in treating this like a road trip, never deviating from the guide books that tell you where to stop and what to see.

We were pleased with our choice of stops; we had another beautiful anchorage to ourselves, and another short day. Satisfied that we had resolved the depth sounder problem, we spent the time cleaning up the installation, neatly dressing the cable from the transducer to the instrument itself, and tying it in with cable ties to the other bundles of wiring that passed through the engine compartment. While in there, I noticed a steady trickle of water from the seawater pump for the engine cooling system. Puzzled, I took a closer look. I had rebuilt that pump while we were in Norfolk; in fact, it had been our justification for an extra night in the marina.

Thinking that perhaps I had forgotten to put sealant on the cover plate gasket, I removed the cover plate and cleaned it thoroughly, putting it back with a new gasket and sealant. I started the engine and ran it for a few minutes, watching as the trickle resumed. We finished installing the cable to the depth sounder transducer and closed everything up again, having used up the time afforded by our early stop.

I mixed a drink and settled in the cockpit to enjoy the last bit of the warm, Indian summer afternoon. Leslie sat beside me as we watched the deer coming out to feed along the banks in the waning light. The pungent aroma of freshly cut pine filled the air as the light breeze shifted. We looked upwind and across the river, seeking the source, finally spotting a barge, partially loaded with pine logs, no doubt destined for a sawmill or a paper mill. Our eyes were drawn back closer to hand by the cry of an osprey circling not far from us. In typical raptor fashion, the wings folded and the large bird streaked toward the surface, pulling up just as its extended talons broke the surface of the water. In a split second, the beating of the powerful wings lifted the bird and a freshly caught, foot-long fish. The osprey flew purposefully toward big nest in a nearby treetop, dinner dangling below.

"What a great life this is," Leslie, the eternal optimist, remarked.

I was thinking about that pump, myself. I was pretty sure it was leaking from the shaft seal, and I didn't have a spare seal. I also knew that the normal rebuild kits didn't include that seal. "At least tomorrow we'll be in Beaufort. I can probably order a seal if there's a Volvo dealer there," I responded.

"You need to enjoy what we have. There's always going to be something broken on the boat; it's no different from a house or a car. We'll cope; there's nothing you can't fix."

I gave her a forced smile, knowing that she was right about the boat, and glad that her confidence in my mechanical aptitude comforted one of us, at least.

Beaufort, N.C.

We had a pleasant, uneventful trip to Beaufort in the company of just a few boats. We had gotten an early start, and we reasoned that most of the boats which stopped in Adams Creek weren't moving yet. It's a relatively short trip to Beaufort, so they were probably sleeping in. We arrived in Beaufort a little after lunchtime and took a quick look at the anchorage off the town. It was crowded, and a swift tidal current ran through it. There were other places to anchor, but we needed to be close to town, and once again, we had to disable the engine for a while to repair that pump. Unhappy at the prospect of spending the money to stay in yet another marina, we knew it was the right decision. Reluctantly, Leslie called the City Marina on the radio and made arrangements.

As we secured the boat in her slip, the couple from St. Michael's pulled in a couple of slips away from us. We were all pleased to see one another again, and we spent a few minutes visiting. We agreed to go out for dinner to an inexpensive place they remembered from their Waterway trip 15 years earlier, and Leslie and I took off to walk the mile or so to the other big marina in town, where the Volvo Marine Diesel dealer was located.

We enjoyed the hike, and the parts manager at the marina was helpful, but he didn't have the pump seals in stock. To further complicate things, Volvo had used a couple of different pumps on the model engine that we had. I studied the parts diagram over the manager's shoulder, and the two pumps looked identical, but the part numbers were different. He could order the seals and get them in two days, but we didn't know which ones we needed.

Stymied, we returned to the boat and I removed the pump. I noticed that it was an aftermarket, replacement pump, rather than a Volvo part, which was not surprising. Our engine was 20 years old. It was too late in the day to return to the Volvo dealer, so I used our cell phone to call the parts manager. The good news was that the pump we had was a standard brand, for which he could order parts, but the problem was that there were two versions, just as for the Volvo part. We agreed that I would return tomorrow with pump in hand so that we could figure out what to do.

We went to dinner with our friends and found that the restaurant, which they remembered as inexpensive but good, had turned into an upscale place. Our friends consulted with the manager and learned that it was still run by the same people, with the same cook, so we decided to try it. The meal was outstanding, and the service was great. Our friends blanched when they saw the bill, but Leslie and I had no regrets. Our budget was blown anyway, at this point. When we had gone through our mail in Elizabeth City and reviewed our bank statement and credit card bills, we had found that we were spending more than our entire monthly budget just on meals in restaurants; we needed to break that habit in the near future, or contemplate going back to work at some point. We weren't spending more than we had in our former lives, but we no longer had our former incomes, either. We knew we would eventually get things under control; meanwhile, we would make the best of this unexpectedly expensive learning curve.

Early the next morning, we walked back to the Volvo dealer. After the parts manager and I studied the pump and the parts drawings in the manufacturer's parts list for a while, neither of us could tell which pump we had in front of us. "How much would it cost to..." I started to ask, as he interrupted with "Why not..."

"... order both versions of the seal?" we asked each other in unison.

"The seals are less than a dollar each. Overnight shipping will cost about $15 bucks," he said.

"Okay. A rebuild takes four seals, so order eight of each part number," I said. I wanted a spare set of seals in our parts locker; this was the sort of failure that started as a nuisance but could escalate quickly.

We left feeling confident that our pump problem would soon be solved. We began to explore the town a little bit, taking a different route back to the boat. We talked as we walked, discussing the unexpected difficulties we were encountering. It was tempting to think that our problems were related to the age of our boat, but we had learned from some of the other folks we had met that most of them were having the same sort of difficulties. New boats, still under warranty, had things that went wrong and people were stranded waiting for parts, or service, or both. Warranty claims were just another aggravation, often complicating and delaying repairs.

We realized that we were more fortunate than most, thanks to my years of experience with all things mechanical and electrical. I had paid my way through college and graduate school working at various jobs ranging from repairing machinery in a paper mill to building and repairing laboratory instruments, so my skills were well-honed, if a bit dated. I had always enjoyed that sort of work; at one point many years ago, my hobby had been rebuilding and restoring antique cars. More recently, tinkering with the boat on the weekends had been a secondary hobby in addition to sailing.

What I was experiencing now was different, though. Back then, whether doing the work for pay or for my own relaxation, I could put down my tools and walk away at the end of a day. Whatever I was repairing wasn't essential to my life in the way that the boat had recently become. Before, I could choose to work on a project or work on something else; I might have to find another way to make income, but my personal stake in the results of my labor didn't seem as great as it did now with the boat. Now I didn't feel that I had a choice.

If I chose not to work on the pump, the marina charges would accrue while I did something more enjoyable. Or, if we happened to be out in the middle of nowhere and I didn't fix the problem, we would be stuck in the middle of nowhere until we ran out of groceries. I could pay somebody else to do the work, but that just opened the door to more problems, as we were learning from the experiences of others. I was feeling more pressure and anxiety than I had anticipated when I made the decision to retire early and go sailing.

"But it still beats working," Leslie said.

"Maybe, but not by much," was my response.

****

Right out of college, I had been hired on a fast-track management development program with a large corporation. The

program was intended to take the company's pick of college
graduates and groom them for rapid advancement to the executive
ranks. It was a well-run program, as those things went, but it was
by design stressful and had a high failure rate. The company was
ultimately benign, though, and put a lot of thought and effort into
helping the program participants learn to cope with the
requirements.

One of the requirements for success in the program, and as
I would learn over the years, in life in general, was the ability to
thrive in a rapidly changing environment. One of the other goals of
the program was to ensure that people who reached the executive
ranks had hands-on experience in all the critical aspects of the
company's operations. To do that, program participants were given
a new job assignment in a different discipline every six to 18
months, and were expected to outperform the people who had
been doing similar jobs for their entire careers. Considerable
counseling went along with this, and one of the things that I learned
that has always served me well was the pattern of a person's
reactions to a new job. There is a predictable series of emotional
reactions that is remarkably consistent, and success required being
able to recognize and deal with those emotions as they occurred.

That night after dinner, I thought about the conversation
that Leslie and I had earlier, and I realized that I had just hit one of
the emotional thresholds that I had been taught to recognize so
long ago. When I first got this new 'job,' I was euphoric. Retire
early and go sailing – of course it was a new job – I just hadn't
thought of it that way before. I had achieved a lifelong goal, but I
had also taken on new challenges in a new environment. Now that I
had worked at it for six months, (and six months, plus or minus just

a little, was a surprisingly consistent period for most employees to hit this threshold) I knew a bit more about what the job involved than I had when I was in that initial period of euphoria. Inevitably, there were parts of the job that I didn't like, and there were challenges that I wasn't expecting and wasn't sure I could willingly meet, even if I didn't doubt my ability. After six months on a new job, an employee is vulnerable; I knew that from my own experience through many career changes, and from years of hiring and managing people. I recognized it now in my own emotional reaction to the setbacks we were experiencing in our cruising life.

I didn't like the situation that I was in any better for having grasped what was happening, but I did know that if I continued to work at it, my state of mind would improve as I began to adjust my expectations and alter the parts of my environment that I could improve. I felt much better about that damned pump now. I was ready to fix it and go on to encounter the next obstacle. The whole reason for embarking on this adventure was to find new challenges and new stimuli. It shouldn't have been a surprise that a lot of them were mundane.

Exploring Beaufort and Our Changes in Perspective

Most waterfront towns along the East Coast date back to the early colonial days. Many are small backwaters now, but once they were hubs of commerce. They all have fascinating histories, and a lot of them have museums to help illustrate their stories. Beaufort, North Carolina, is a prime example. While we waited for our parts to arrive, we availed ourselves of the North Carolina Maritime Museum. Through the broad scope of its exhibits, we quickly became grounded in the history of the area.

Beaufort and the adjacent town of Morehead City, (Bō-fert and Mow-haid City, in the local vernacular) have ready access to the sea via a stable, natural inlet on a stretch of shoreline that runs in an east-west direction. Unlike most of the other inlets in North Carolina's outer banks, this one is mostly protected from the ravages of North Atlantic storms by its orientation and its location relative to Cape Lookout, the middle one of the three North Carolina capes that stretch their treacherous shoals far out into the Atlantic. Cape Fear is the southernmost, and the notorious Cape Hatteras is the northern one. The shape of the shoreline provides little natural protection to the inlets near the other two capes, but Beaufort's inlet is tucked well up inside the concave stretch of shoreline, and so has been less prone to shoaling over the centuries than the other two.

As a result of its naturally protected entrance and its location on the central part of the North Carolina coast, Beaufort was an important trading port early in the history of our country. As we walked around the carefully restored historic district with its old houses, many now small inns, we were magically transported back in time. With help from the guidebooks and museum exhibits, it was easy to imagine what life in Beaufort had been like in its early days.

As the morning passed, we began to shed our fall clothing. The heavy wool sweaters that felt good when we woke up on the boat were hot by mid-morning. Based on the morning's weather forecast we had not expected such benign temperatures today. We stopped in a coffee shop for an espresso, and while the proprietor filled our order, she asked if it was warming up outside. When we agreed that it was quite warm and expressed our surprise, she explained that Beaufort was usually much warmer than the surrounding area because of its proximity to the sea and the Gulf Stream.

We realized then what she meant. We had been casually studying the Gulf Stream recently, in anticipation of crossing it in the near future to go to the Bahamas. The Gulf Stream waters are quite warm; usually in the low 80 degree range, as a result of the stream's origin in the tropics. The swift current is like a river of warm water flowing through the much colder Atlantic waters as it skirts the Atlantic coast. As the Gulf Stream squeezes through the narrow, 40-mile-wide gap between the western Bahamas and south Florida, its western edge is only a mile or two off the coast. Because the coastline falls away to the west as the stream flows north, by the time it is opposite Savannah and Charleston, the Stream's western edge is closer to 100 miles offshore, and the Stream itself has spread out to a width that sometimes reaches 100 miles. As the Stream continues its northerly course, the shoreline comes back out to meet it. In the vicinity of Cape Lookout, it is again only a few miles offshore.

The current in the Stream is strong, moving at three to five miles per hour. Slow-moving vessels traveling north have taken advantage of the push from the Gulf Stream since the early colonial era. This is another reason for the early prosperity of the Beaufort area; its proximity to the Gulf Stream put it very close to the major north-south commercial 'highway' of the colonial and post colonial periods.

Ships were not alone in taking advantage of the Gulf Stream. Marine life is transported from the tropics by the flow, providing a bounty of seafood for the fishing fleets, and fishermen based along this stretch of shoreline didn't have to venture far out to sea to find rich pickings. We learned from the museums that the beach along Shackleford Banks, a low, sandy island stretching between Beaufort Inlet and Cape Lookout, was littered with seashells normally only found in Caribbean waters, as well as all manner of interesting flotsam deposited by the Gulf Stream as it swirled along near the shore.

One advantage to staying in the marina was that they kept a fleet of loaner cars for the use of visitors. The cars were drivable but in rough shape, although they were adequate for short trips. There were several, but the cars were popular with the cruising crowd. After several attempts at scheduling, we managed to secure one of them for an afternoon grocery shopping expedition with the couple from St. Michael's. The car was of great benefit, as the grocery store would have been too far to walk carrying the amount of food we needed. We stocked up; once we left Beaufort, full-line grocery stores would be scarce for several days, at least within walking distance of the Waterway.

****

Since we had arrived in Beaufort, we had been in touch with a former coworker of mine who had moved to Raleigh, North Carolina, just a short drive from Beaufort. He and his wife drove down to spend a few hours with us, coincidentally on the day our pump parts arrived. While I took advantage of his car to pick up those seals for the cooling water pump and some other odds and ends from a marine supply store a few miles away in Morehead City, our wives toured the quaint shops in downtown Beaufort. As we compared notes with them over lunch in one of the many restaurants along the waterfront, Leslie and I realized how much our lives had changed in a short period.

We saw how pale our friends looked compared to our own rough, salt-bleached, sun-bronzed appearance. But more surprisingly to us, we noticed how much less we had in common with them now. They were both still working, filled with news of former colleagues and the frustrations of earning a living. Our frustrations were centered on more elemental things: what would the weather do for the next few days as we tried to get farther south, what boat problem would we have to deal with next, and how far south would we have to sail before we found another grocery store within walking distance. They had been reading the posts on our website, and the woman had already remarked to Leslie that we seemed to spend an awful lot of time working on the boat and going grocery shopping.

We noticed a big difference in our choices for lunch; they were worried about staying on their diets, but we had voracious appetites and had lost weight since we moved aboard the boat. Walking to the grocery store and carrying your purchases home has some benefits.

After lunch, we walked our friends back to their car, waving as they drove back to their workaday lives. Strolling back to the boat, Leslie remarked on her shopping excursion with my friend's wife. "She spent all her time looking at knickknacks for their house and clothes for work."

"What did you look at?" I was thinking of how much she had enjoyed running her women's clothing store, and how fascinated she had been with the fashion industry. I thought her shopping trip might have made her nostalgic for what had been her dream job.

"A sweater. I thought I could use another one, since that's all we've been wearing."

"Find any?" I asked, still worried.

"No. They were all too dressy and expensive; I need something practical."

I was wondering whether I heard a little wistfulness in her tone, but before I could probe that, she continued.

"I was bored with shopping; we need to get that pump put back together and get out of the marina. You get the parts okay?"

Beaufort to Mile Hammock Bay

We were up and away early, rising before dawn to take advantage of the slack period in the tidal current that was ripping through the marina. Entering and leaving Beaufort's town docks with the swift cross-current flowing is treacherous; *Play Actor's* long, deep underwater profile limits her maneuverability in such situations. Besides, we were past being ready to move on and leaving before sunrise suited us.

We had outsmarted ourselves, thinking that since we were stuck waiting for parts anyway, Beaufort would be a good place to finish up a lingering tax matter. I had asked the accountant to send the necessary papers via Federal Express overnight delivery, but neither of us realized at the time that it was Friday when I called him, and Federal Express didn't deliver to our marina address on Saturday. As a result, we had spent an idle weekend in Beaufort, waiting for the package to arrive on Monday so that I could sign the papers and send them on. Ties to our old life complicated our new one more than we had thought they would.

By the time the sun was above the horizon, we had left the Beaufort-Morehead City waterfront behind and were just entering Bogue Sound, a two-mile-wide by 20-mile-long stretch of water that ranges in depth from one to two feet, for the most part. A thin strip of low, sandy barrier island called the Bogue Bank separates Bogue Sound from the ocean and boasts a number of beach resorts. This stretch of the Waterway doesn't look like a ditch; it's quite pretty with broad expanses of clear, calm water punctuated by innumerable small, sandy islands, some large enough to support a bit of vegetation. In warm weather, it would doubtless be a paradise for folks with small, shallow-draft boats, offering everyone their own private beach. It was too cold for that when we went through the Sound, but there were plenty of small, outboard-powered fishing boats, their occupants working the endless shoals for sport.

Although it didn't look like a ditch, it certainly felt like one as we carefully steered *Play Actor* along the well-marked, twelve-foot-deep, dredged channel through the shallows. We were headed almost due west for this stretch, with the early morning sun shining brightly over our shoulders, providing a surreal, stark look to the view ahead. As the sun got a little higher, the deeper, darker water of the channel was clearly visible between the shallow, pale green expanses to either side. The details of navigation markers, low-lying sandy islands, and small boats were brought into sharp relief by the bright light from behind us.

Before the Corps of Engineers dredged this channel, this inviting stretch of water wouldn't have been navigable to any boat much bigger than a rowboat, although it had no doubt been an important source of fresh seafood since pre-colonial days. Now it supports a fair amount of barge traffic, hauling commodities of various sorts. Before dredging, commercial traffic would have followed the shoreline on the ocean-side of the Bogue Bank from Beaufort Inlet to Bogue Inlet at Swansboro. The distance is a little over 30 miles, via either the offshore or the inland route, but in contrast to the stable, deep, all-weather inlet at Beaufort, Bogue Inlet is shallow, shifting, and treacherous, so this leg of the Waterway is commercially important.

When we were planning today's route, we thought we would anchor for the night in the Swansboro Channel, right in 'downtown' Swansboro, North Carolina, but when we got there it was mid-morning, a bit too early to stop for the day, given that we had just idled away the weekend and were well rested. We took a look at the charts and saw that by early afternoon, we would be in the vicinity of the New River Inlet. Just north of the inlet, there was a large, dredged basin called Mile Hammock Bay, a part of the Marine Corps base at Camp LeJeune, which looked to be a serviceable anchorage for a night. Beyond Mile Hammock Bay, we didn't see an attractive spot to anchor before Wrightsville Beach, which was too far for us to reach in daylight. We decided to try Mile Hammock Bay, although the entrance channel from the Waterway was shown as being too shallow for our depth. The bay itself looked deep enough, and we would arrive a couple of hours before high tide, which should add enough depth to the entrance channel to allow us to enter.

Finding a satisfactory anchorage on the Waterway is more involved than we had expected. There is traffic of all sorts in the dredged channel at all hours of the night and day, so to stop for the night, we had to find a spot that was out of the way of traffic, deep enough for our six-foot draft, and wide enough to let us swing in a circle of roughly 200 feet in diameter at the whim of the wind and current. Anchoring a boat isn't like parking a car; to allow the anchor to dig in and hold, it's necessary to let out enough rope, or, in our case, chain, to equal four to seven times the depth of the water; this length of the anchor chain is called 'scope,' and without sufficient scope to keep the pull of the chain on the anchor near horizontal, there is a risk of pulling the anchor out and dragging it across the bottom, hence that 200-foot circle. Then there is the issue of the quality of the bottom itself. An anchor digs into thick, sticky mud or soft sand readily and holds well. In some areas of swift current, the bottom has been scoured down to a hard, smooth substrate, and an anchor won't penetrate to enough depth to hold the boat.

We've also learned that a reasonable day's travel is no more than 50 miles unless we want to run at night, which is certainly possible, but it's not attractive. We're doing this to enjoy the scenery. Adding the 50-mile constraint to the requirements for a reasonable nighttime anchorage resulted in a need for more planning than we had expected. That said, we enjoyed the trip to Mile Hammock Bay more than any of our recent days along the Waterway. The boat was behaving well, nothing was broken, the scenery was beautiful, and the weather was idyllic. Our life was unfolding as we had thought it would, and we felt fortunate to be where we were.

****

Our night in Mile Hammock Bay was quiet, although we'd read that it wasn't always so. The Marines use Mile Hammock Bay to launch amphibious assault vehicles, chunky, tank-like machines with big, powerful, noisy diesel engines and clanking tracks. There were no maneuvers during our stay, and the only other human occupants were on cruising boats like us. We were awakened by the noise of our neighbors starting their day's journey south, and as soon as we finished our breakfast, we joined the parade of boats headed for Wrightsville Beach, some 40 miles farther along the Ditch.

Mile Hammock Bay to Wrightsville Beach

Although decidedly ditch-like, this segment of the Waterway turned out to be very pretty. In contrast to the parts of the route that had been literally cut through solid ground and Bogue Sound, with its inviting vistas of open, protected water, the channel along this part of the Waterway is dredged through marshland that fills the mile-wide space between the barrier island and the mainland. The marsh was teeming with wildlife of all sorts. We spotted raccoons, otter, deer, and innumerable birds as we passed. The air was rich with the tangy, salt marsh smell that evoked pleasant childhood memories for me, recollections of fishing and exploring the salt marsh farther south.

Several chokepoints in the form of drawbridges kept the all the boats together. We were effectively traveling in a convoy, and the channel was narrow enough to discourage faster boats from passing slower ones. There was adequate room, but because of the natural tendency to steer down the middle of the channel, passing required some attention on the part of both skippers, and to us, there was little incentive to pass slightly slower boats, since we would all have to wait for the next drawbridge to open anyway. The bridge tenders make an effort to keep both road and water traffic flowing reasonably smoothly, and opening and closing a bridge takes several minutes, during which no traffic of either variety can pass. So, if the bridge tender sees a line of boats stretching back for a mile or more, she will wait until most are gathered near the bridge, waiting for the draw to open.

By now, all the southbound boats know the routine, having negotiated a number of drawbridges. Nevertheless, some people are unable to restrain their compulsion to be "first," particularly the ones who are on faster boats. As we idle along comfortably, keeping pace with our neighbors, sipping coffee as we admire the ever changing vista, we listen to the radio traffic generated as the "type A" captains call the slower boats to request that they pull over and throttle back. Some are belligerent and impatient; we wonder why they are doing this. Clearly, they aren't enjoying it. They've developed their own semi-literate language, too, which we find amusing. We noticed earlier that the less experienced people were at using the VHF radio, the more pompous they sounded. We laughed out loud at one obviously frustrated man. We heard him time after time, using the same impatient tone.

Most people had their attention focused on the water immediately in front of them as they steered; that's where the hazards to be avoided were. They would glance over a shoulder occasionally to check behind them, but common sense and the nautical rules of the road both give the right of way to a vessel being overtaken. If another boat is approaching from behind, the overtaking boat has the burden of not ramming the boat in front. There are prescribed protocols for overtaking in close quarters where a danger of collision exists, specifying whistle signals to be used by the overtaking vessel to request *permission* to pass the vessel being overtaken. The vessel being overtaken has the right to specify on which side it wishes the overtaking vessel to pass and further, the right to refuse permission to the overtaking vessel if the skipper of the vessel that is being overtaken deems passing to be dangerous. After all, the boat in front is in a better position to see what hazards might be coming up. Whistle signals are required, although *both* vessels *may* agree to negotiate passing situations using the radio.

Many of our fellow cruisers appeared to have learned their seamanship in high school driver's education, though, and the finer points of managing encounters with another vessel were lost on them, as evidenced by the following episode.

"Slow sailboat in front of me, this is the trawler *Klondike* requesting that you slow down and move over so that I can have a safe 'passage.' Over."

Besides the tone of voice and the pompous use of 'passage,' which to most sailors connotes a trip, usually offshore, *Klondike's* radio call was unclear. If *Klondike* had said, "*Windblown, Windblown*, this is *Klondike,* requesting permission to pass on your port side," it would have been much more likely to get a favorable response. Notice that there is significantly more information in the properly worded call, including which slow sailboat *Klondike* wants to pass, and upon which side. With the call that *Klondike* actually made, *Windblown* had no clue as to which boat *Klondike* wanted to pass, because even if the skipper of *Windblown* had been looking backward, *Klondike*, like many other boats, only has a name on the stern, where only the boats behind her can see it.

After a few seconds with no response from "slow sailboat in front of me," we heard, "This is *Klondike,* you jerk. I'm passing you on the left. Move it or lose it." There was still no response, either because *Windblown* didn't have a radio (It's not required – that's why whistle signals are the law.) or because he didn't realize he was the particular "slow sailboat."

We watched this play out several times, including once when we were the "slow sailboat." *Klondike* was one of several boats that we saw exhibiting that sort of behavior. We could tell that they weren't enjoying the trip and we were glad of it. They didn't deserve to enjoy it; they should have bought motor homes instead of boats. It was immensely satisfying to most of us to find the people in a hurry waiting at the next drawbridge as the rest of us took our time catching up. Remembering the commercial seamen who worked the Waterway down south when I was growing up, I speculated that it wouldn't be too long before someone forcibly adjusted *Klondike's* attitude.

Drawbridges and jerks notwithstanding, we made it to Wrightsville Beach in the early afternoon. We stopped at a marina to top up our diesel and water tanks on the way to the anchorage. That done, we got ourselves settled and had a mid-afternoon coffee break, enjoying the warm, pleasant breeze that brought the distinctive aroma of the sea from the other side of the barrier island. Although most of the boats in the morning's convoy had kept going, the anchorage was moderately crowded. We soon got a call on the cell phone from our friends from St. Michael's, who had surreptitiously watched us anchor. They had left Beaufort while we were waiting for the pump parts. We dropped the dinghy and rowed over to visit, learning that they had spent a few days enjoying Wrightsville Beach. They were planning to move on in the morning.

They filled us in on the grocery stores, marine supply stores, and restaurants in Wrightsville Beach. It all sounded grand, but we had wanderlust, having spent too long sitting still during our extended stop in Beaufort. We would continue our trip in the morning as well.

Wrightsville Beach to the Shallotte River

Our route south from Wrightsville Beach took us through Masonboro Sound and Myrtle Grove Sound, both of which resembled yesterday's arrow-straight, dredged route through the marshlands that lie between the barrier islands and the mainland. Just south of Carolina Beach inlet, which is ten miles north of Cape Fear, the marshlands disappear and there is a small, shallow basin off the town of Carolina Beach. Like most beach towns along this coast, Carolina Beach is on the barrier island.

At Carolina Beach the Waterway makes a sharp turn to the west, following a man-made one-and-a-half mile long canal through relatively high ground to the Cape Fear River. Snow's Cut, as this canal is known, is infamous for its strong tidal currents. As *Play Actor* slogged through the foul current, slowed down from her normal six to seven mile-per-hour speed to about two miles per hour, we had ample time to read the graffiti on the abutments of the 65-foot-high bridge which spans Snow's Cut. The most memorable message was "Die, rich scum!" No longer feeling rich, we didn't take that personally.

When we finally left the cut and broke loose from the current that had been holding us back, we saw the biggest expanse of open water since the Chesapeake Bay. We realized then that we had been feeling a bit of claustrophobia in the Ditch after the novelty had worn off. Our attention was focused on picking out the last few channel markers that would take us the last mile to the seemingly boundless main channel of the Cape Fear River, so we didn't notice the small, nondescript white sailboat circling near the mouth of the cut until we were about 50 yards from it.

"*Play Actor, Play Actor!* Help us please! Help!" a panic stricken woman's voice blared from the speaker of our VHF radio.

"This is *Play Actor*. Who's calling us, please, and what can we do to help you?" I responded, quickly scanning our immediate area, seeing only the one boat close enough to read our name.

"We're the boat just off your right side," the woman said. "We need help, please."

They were afloat and under control, so we thought perhaps there was a medical emergency, but we wondered why they didn't call the Coast Guard, as we were well within range of any kind of official help they might require.

"How can we help you?" I asked again.

"We don't know where to go next," the woman said, voice quavering.

"Where do you want to go?" I asked, suppressing a chuckle as I realized that, perhaps for the first time, they had to actually use a bit of skill to navigate, as opposed to following what had amounted to a road that required no decisions as to route for the last several hundred miles. There was a broad range of choices of direction here.

"Florida. We want to go to Florida," she said, "and then the Bahamas."

"Okay. That's the way we're headed," I said. "Just follow us."

"Oh, thank you so much," the woman said, her relief immediately apparent in her suddenly melodious voice.

"You're welcome. Where have you come from?"

"Brooklyn. Thanks again." This was a man's voice, thick with a Brooklyn accent.

The boat surged forward as we passed it, taking up a position uncomfortably close to our stern. Leslie and I both were amazed that this couple had managed to get themselves into such a situation. We laughingly speculated that they had road maps from the American Automobile Association, instead of a proper set of nautical charts. They held their position right on our stern for the next couple of hours as we followed the broad Cape Fear River down to Southport, North Carolina. A mile or so farther south, the river flows into the ocean at Bald Head Inlet, a good, all-weather inlet, which serves ocean-going ships bound to and from the inland port of Wilmington, North Carolina. At Southport, the Waterway turns to the west and follows a dredged cut just inland from the ocean. The cut connects a series of small estuaries with several inlets that are only suitable for small boats in settled weather.

From perusing the charts, we had not been able to pick an anchorage for the night, so we had decided to keep going until we found a spot that perhaps didn't show up on the charts. Through all this the couple from Brooklyn stayed right on our stern, determined to follow the leader. They never identified themselves by boat name, so Leslie and I started referring to them as *"Lost Boat"* in our conversations about them.

About eight hours after leaving Wrightsville Beach, we heard our friends from St. Michael's call the Holden Beach marina, which we had passed 20 minutes earlier, and arrange for a slip for the night. We kept going, periodically slowing down and edging cautiously into any streams off the channel that looked promising, but we found nowhere to anchor until we reached the Shallotte River. The chart showed a relatively deep but narrow unmarked channel leading from the Waterway up the Shallotte, so we planned to find our way into the mouth of the river by using our depth sounder to locate the channel. Once we got through the narrow entrance, it appeared that there would be adequate room for us to anchor for the night.

As we approached the river, the sun was low and the visibility was poor. We slowed down gradually to avoid being run down by *Lost Boat*, still close on our stern. As we drew even with the wide, deceptively inviting mouth of the Shallotte River, we edged to the side of the channel, watching the depth sounder closely for evidence that we were near the end of the sandbar that we knew all but closed off the river entrance. Once we could clearly see up the river, *Lost Boat* turned sharply to the right, promptly running hard aground on the bar with its stern in the edge of the Waterway channel. We kept half an eye on *Lost Boat* as we felt our way past the bar and into the deeper water of the river's unmarked channel. *Lost Boat* made no effort to get off the sandbar; we saw the man drop his anchor straight down off the bow, and then they turned on their anchor light. As we anchored 100 yards up the river, a local shrimp boat, 50 or 60 feet long, turned into the river and gave us a friendly wave as we sat relaxing in the cockpit. We watched as the shrimper followed the narrow, intricately winding, channel up the river and out of sight. Clearly, these were familiar waters to him.

As we went to bed, we talked again about the couple on *Lost Boat*, hoping that they didn't get run down by a tug during the night. At least, they were showing a bright white anchor light at the masthead, so they weren't invisible, although they were in the edge of the narrow channel. During the night, a violent storm blew through with some rain and winds of 35 to 40 knots. We both woke up and went on deck to make sure that *Play Actor* stayed put. Dragging the anchor would have surely put us aground, as we were surrounded by shallows, even though we sat in about 15 feet of water. Satisfied that our anchor was holding, we looked for *Lost Boat's* anchor light, but couldn't find it. We went back to bed and fell asleep as the remnant of the storm blew itself out.

Shallotte River, N.C. to Myrtle Beach, S.C.

Awake at dawn, I made a cup of coffee and went up to sit in the cockpit, hoping that Leslie could sleep in. We were expecting a short day, as we planned to stop at Barefoot Landing, a huge discount shopping center at Myrtle Beach, South Carolina. Like the North Carolina welcome center in the Dismal Swamp Canal, Barefoot Landing has a public dock along the Waterway and a front entrance for automobile traffic on U.S. Highway 17. It's an easy 25-mile trip from the Shallotte River, and Leslie didn't sleep well because of the storm.

Sipping my coffee, I noticed that *Lost Boat* was missing. I doubted that they had left already; it wasn't even fully light yet, and they didn't seem the type to leave before daylight. I picked up the binoculars and made a careful sweep of the area, finally spotting them a mile or so up the river. They appeared to be resting easily, not wrecked in the marsh or obviously aground. Sure that their anchor had dragged during the storm, I was amazed that they had successfully negotiated the unmarked river channel in the dark.

By the time I had finished my coffee, Leslie was awake and making breakfast. We took our time, eating in the cockpit, waiting to see if *Lost Boat* could find her way out of the river without going aground. When we had finished eating and prepared a thermos of coffee without seeing any sign of life on *Lost Boat*, we decided to be on our way. Once again, we were out of synch with the rest of the crowd; we traveled by ourselves through the beautiful coastal lowlands, cautiously crossing several of the small inlets on our way to Myrtle Beach.

The swift tidal currents around the inlets result in constantly shifting shoals where the inlet channels intersect the Waterway. Although marked by buoys, the shoals change more quickly than the buoys can be moved, so each inlet crossing is a source of stress. Grounding the boat on one of these shoals isn't especially dangerous, but it could result in hours of delay while waiting for the tide to rise, or, worst case, waiting for a towboat to come.

We had learned that there were a couple of franchised towing services that worked along the Waterway. For a modest annual fee, they sold towing insurance, much like the American Automobile Association, and we knew that a lot of people bought policies. We had heard that without a policy, the hourly rate for pulling a boat like ours off of a sandbar or mud bank could run into the hundreds of dollars. As a lifelong denizen of the Ditch, I was content to rely on my navigational skill to avoid running aground, confident as well that if we did run aground, I had the know-how to get us afloat again without assistance.

We had noticed over the last couple of days that at every inlet, there were towboats hovering nearby like vultures waiting for the traffic to clear around road kill. We learned to look for them as early warning indicators of shoal water ahead, and their presence helped us to avoid running aground. After all, tugs with heavily laden barges drew as much or more water than our six feet, and they were at least three or four times as wide as *Play Actor*. Where they could go, we could go, we reasoned. "Think like a barge," I counseled myself, as we approached the shallows around the inlets. It served us well, but there was still an element of anxiety as we watched the vultures watching us hungrily.

Just after we crossed the Little River Inlet, we were passed by a large, fast moving powerboat. As it disappeared around the next bend, we heard the skipper calling the Little River Swing Bridge to request an opening; we knew we were few minutes from the bridge. We heard the bridge tender answer.

"Good mornin' captain. Did you pass any other southbound boats in the last few minutes? I'd like to make sure we get as many folks through the opening as we can; helps with the road traffic."

"Good morning, bridgetender. There's nobody behind us," the skipper of the fast powerboat answered.

Annoyed, I picked up the microphone. "Little River swing bridge, this is *Play Actor.*"

"Good mornin', *Play Actor.* This is the bridge. How can I help?"

"We're a sailboat about five minutes from you, southbound. We'll want an opening, please."

"You got it, captain. I'll wait fer ye. I can see yer mast over the marsh grass. Reckon this here feller's in a hurry, but he'll have to wait a minute. This here twistin' an' a turnin' the bridge span ever' few minutes jest don't git it. Thanks fer callin'."

We reached Barefoot Landing early in the afternoon and found that the entire 500-foot-long public dock was occupied with boats. As we studied the situation, a couple on a boat slightly larger than ours waved us over and encouraged us to tie up to them, which we did. We visited with them for a few minutes and learned that this was their second trip down the Ditch. They brought out their charts, showing us their favorite anchorages on the way south. As we were chatting, our friends from St. Michael's appeared, followed closely by *Lost Boat.* We excused ourselves from our new friends and close neighbors, and went ashore to help get the two new arrivals secured alongside a couple of other boats a bit farther down the dock.

Once they were both tied up, we approached *Lost Boat.* "How in the world did you find your way up the Shallotte River in the dark in that storm?" I asked.

"That was the Shallotte River?" the man responded. "We just woke up there. Guess it's better to be lucky than good, huh?"

"I guess," I said. "How'd you find the channel on your way out?"

"No problem. Just followed a shrimp boat. When we got to the Waterway again, we just got in line."

I nodded. "Glad it worked out," I said.

Privately, I recalled a saying that I first heard from a crusty old sergeant when I was a newly commissioned Army officer. "Don't worry too much, son. Things mostly come out all right. God looks after fools, drunks, and the United States of America," he had advised me, and he was right, I think.

Defective Bibles and the Waccamaw River

We left Barefoot Landing early in the morning of the following day. By late afternoon on the day of our arrival, the dock was layered three-deep with boats for its entire length. We were sandwiched into the middle file, and we had been worried about extricating ourselves, having heard from several near-neighbors that they were planning to stay a few days. We needn't have worried; most of the cruising community turns in early and gets up with the sun, it seems, and by the time we were ready to leave, people were happily shuffling boats around to make way for those of us who were moving on.

We wondered as we left what attracted people to stay for an extended period. We had spent a couple of hours yesterday afternoon walking around the mall with our friends. There was a broad selection of stores, most selling things that we didn't need at attractive prices. Two stores drew our attention. One sold tools of all sorts, and the other was a Bible factory outlet. Given my hands-on approach to all things mechanical, it's no wonder that the tool store caught my eye, but a Bible factory outlet? We had a Bible aboard, and didn't need another, but we were enthralled by the notion. What did they sell? Overstocks? Defective Bibles? We had to know, so we went in and browsed the merchandise. Indeed, they had both overstocks and defective Bibles in all price ranges. The defects ranged from problems with the binding, to misprints, to Bibles with missing pages or books. Some had sections that were upside down. The irony of a defective Bible being offered for sale at a reduced price fascinated us. The incremental cost of a nondefective Bible was insignificant when considered in the context of how long one might use a Bible. "Why would someone buy a defective Bible?" Leslie asked a teenaged sales clerk who had offered to assist us.

The girl shrugged and smiled. "I guess because it's a good price?"

We decided that was why so many of our fellow boaters were staying over. We had watched several people board their boats late yesterday, laden with shopping bags. We wondered where they put all those defective Bibles and other things that they bought because "...it's a good price." It's no wonder so many of them want bigger boats.

We didn't buy anything but a good Italian dinner, which we didn't need, but we felt compelled to spend some money in exchange for the free dockage. As we motored down the last miles of the dredged canal that borders Myrtle Beach, we talked about the retail free-for-all that we had left behind. Leslie made a living in the retail world for years, and she reminded me of one of her sales lines that I've always enjoyed. I made a living in commercial sales, and my sales pitches were usually based on the economic benefit to the customer of buying my product over a competing one. Leslie, however, was quite accustomed to her customers saying, "It's lovely, but I don't need a $500 dress." Her response was, "Of course you don't. Where does need come into this? You look beautiful in the dress; it was made for you."

"But it's a party dress; I don't have anywhere to wear it."

"If you buy that dress, the party will come." Leslie's percentage of sales closed was very high compared to mine.

****

We soon left the canal and entered the Waccamaw River, another pristine natural watercourse that winds its way through primeval cypress swamp, much like the Pasquotank in North Carolina. The Waccamaw, though, feels less confined than the Pasquotank. We were so overcome by the contrast between the Waccamaw and the dredged canals we had traversed for the last few days that we decided to take a break. We were only about three hours south of Barefoot Landing, but we could have been in a different world. The weather was pleasant, and we were getting far enough south to expect reasonably warm days anyway. We eased *Play Actor* into the next likely looking side channel while keeping a careful eye on the depth sounder. We found plenty of water all the way through the oxbow; when it rejoined the main river channel, we turned around. We went back to the center of the bend and dropped the anchor in our own private wildlife sanctuary.

Amazed at the notion that we were only a few minutes by car from the bustle of Barefoot Landing and Myrtle Beach, we sat in the cockpit in our shirtsleeves and finished our coffee. We were entertained by watching and listening to a large, pileated woodpecker hammering away at a dead cypress that stood on the edge of the swampy little island that screened us from the main channel of the river. Although we couldn't see them, we could hear the sounds of the boats going by out in the river. It was so still and quiet that we could hear the people aboard the boats conversing over the soft purr of their engines. Imagining how peaceful it would be tonight when the traffic died down, we congratulated ourselves on our decision.

Once we finished our coffee, we launched the dinghy and rowed ourselves well up into the swamp. Once past the first few trees, we were able to pull the dinghy along by grabbing the low hanging brush. Soon we were in a little pool, perhaps 30 feet across, shaded by the trees, watching the birds chasing insects. We couldn't even see *Play Actor,* although she was no more than 100 yards away. Using a seven-foot oar, we probed the coffee-colored water to test the depth, but even by rolling up my sleeve and adding the length of my arm to that of the oar, I couldn't touch the bottom. Leslie remarked that she was still able to see the tip of the white oar, some nine feet below the surface. The color of the water made the oar look orange, but the water was not at all cloudy. The orange tint of the water comes from the tannic acid that leaches from the trees and is typical of cypress swamps. Back in the days of sail, ship captains prized such water for their fresh water casks, as the tannic acid acted as a preservative and kept the water sweet for extended periods at sea.

Back aboard *Play Actor,* we spent a quiet afternoon reading. Over a leisurely dinner, we discussed whether we should spend another day here. That's a recurring question. Every time we find a special place like this one, we ponder whether to stay or move on. We reminded ourselves that this didn't have to be our only trip on the Waterway; we could make a note of this place as somewhere we wanted to see again and keep moving. We took a look at tomorrow's route and saw that we were just a few hours from Georgetown, South Carolina, which promised a good anchorage and another small, historic town to explore.

We decided to move on in the morning. We were learning to expect that there would always be another beautiful anchorage around the next bend, just as there would always be something else broken or about to break on the boat. With several days of beautiful scenery and no recent boat problems, our life seemed well balanced. That day, I found absolutely nothing attractive about the idea of going back to work; we were living as we had dreamed we would.

Waccamaw River to Georgetown, S.C.

We had breakfast in the cockpit, thoroughly rested after our day off yesterday. We had fallen asleep listening to the sounds of wildlife in the swamp, including the squeals and grunts of feral hogs, the hooting of owls, the ever-present bullfrogs, and the occasional call of a bull alligator. Although far from the nighttime sounds to which we were accustomed, none of this kept us awake. It was a balmy morning, and we lingered over our coffee before retrieving the anchor and motoring back into the river.

Once again, thanks to our whimsical behavior, we were out of step with the crowd. We had heard the wave of boats from the early departure at Barefoot Landing go by while we ate our breakfast, but we felt no compulsion to be part of the group. We enjoyed the rest of the scenic Waccamaw, although it broadened all too quickly for us. We were soon in relatively open water approaching the small seaport of Georgetown.

Georgetown is the best South Carolina port north of Charleston. Where the Sampit River flowed into the Waccamaw, nature formed a small but well-protected harbor. Just past the junction the Waccamaw opens into Winyah Bay, and 12 miles downstream, the Winyah Bay entrance channel provides deep, well-protected access to the sea. Historically, the port of Georgetown was much more important commercially than it is today. In the colonial era, it provided the local indigo plantations with access to the world's markets. A little later, indigo gave way to rice, and Georgetown continued to thrive. By 1840, the area produced almost one-half of the total rice crop of the U.S. and the port of

Georgetown was the third largest shipping port for rice in the world. Today, neither of those commodities is important locally, but Georgetown, with a population of about 9,000 people, has a paper mill and a steel mill; it is still an important seaport.

We had no problem entering Georgetown's harbor, and we quickly found a spot to anchor within two hundred yards of the center of town. We had a quick lunch and launched the dinghy, rowing ashore in just a few minutes. Stepping from the dinghy dock, we found ourselves on an attractive, well-kept main street, lined with shops and restaurants, none of which looked to be tourist traps. Georgetown, although small, appeared to be self-sufficient. This, we suspected, was a quintessential small town, not many of which exist today, at least along the East Coast. We shopped in a neat, well-organized bookstore, where we bought a couple of books that we'd been hunting.

Next door, in an antique shop, we found a set of four demitasse cups that appealed, as we had broken two of our four recently. When we asked the lady in the store about them, she said, "I think she wants $10, but I'll have to call her. We're a co-op; the cups aren't mine." We waited a minute or two, and the woman returned with four matching saucers in hand.

"I was right about the $10, but I'm glad I called her. I didn't know she had the saucers." As she wrapped our purchase carefully in tissue paper, she made polite conversation, asking where we were from. She was fascinated to hear that we were on a boat; although the merchants had sought to publicize their town as an attraction for boaters, they didn't believe that they had generated much interest, she told us. We weren't able to comment on that, although we did tell her that all we had heard about the town was that it offered a protected anchorage between Myrtle Beach and Charleston. She then bemoaned the fact that the outlets in Myrtle Beach ruined the market for local merchants. We were momentarily surprised, having just spent two days getting here from Myrtle Beach. She read our puzzlement after a moment, and smiled. "It's less than an hour by car," she reminded us.

We walked around, window shopping, and decided that we would stay here for an extra day. There was the Rice Museum to explore, along with some buildings of historical interest. Besides, we were getting close to Charleston, and we had some time to kill. It was a little over a week until Thanksgiving, and Leslie's folks were going to spend Thanksgiving week with us in Charleston, so we weren't pressed for time. As we ambled back to the dock where we left the dinghy, we ran into a couple that we recognized from our stay in Elizabeth City. We stopped to chat with them for a few minutes, learning that they had come all the way from Little River Inlet today. They were proud to have covered over 60 miles in a day. They were surprised to learn that we had spent five days covering the same distance, telling us that they would be in Charleston tomorrow night. When we asked if they had some compelling schedule, they shrugged. "No, but this is boring," the man replied. "No sailing, nothing to see. We're ready for the Bahamas." We wished them a swift journey and went home to *Play Actor,* where we washed and put away our new demitasse cups and cooked dinner.

The next day, we methodically walked the streets of Georgetown. It offered an enthralling mix of old, colonial-era buildings and much newer, more modest houses. We picked up a number of brochures at the Chamber of Commerce which gave us an idea of what we were seeing as we strolled through the historic district. We particularly enjoyed seeing the magnificent building that was built for the still-active Winyah Indigo Society in the early 19th century. The Society itself dates back to the early 18th century, when it was formed as a social organization for the wealthy indigo planters in the area.

We spent a good bit of time in the Rice Museum; it was of particular interest to me. As a child, I had spent many a weekend fishing in the canals that had once irrigated rice fields near Savannah. The incredible investment of labor that went into the cultivation of rice along the southeastern coast is still amazing to me. The miles of canals that converted marshland to agricultural use were dug with muscle power; men and mules had excavated all those geometrically perfect, 12-foot-wide, 12-foot-deep trenches, and highly skilled slave labor had constructed the wooden flood gates of native timber to harness the several feet of tidal change to alternately dry and irrigate the fields. The junctions of the canals with tidal streams had been provided with locally made brick seawalls to limit erosion by the tidal current. Many of these structures were so well designed and executed that they were still in place over two hundred years later, although rice had not been actively cultivated in most of the region for a long time. The magnitude of the industry was astounding; the rice culture stretched from this area all the way south to Spanish Florida. It was no wonder that so much of the world's rice was produced here, considering the scope of the construction.

Of equal interest to me was the Maritime Museum, the sole exhibit of which was called the "Brown's Ferry Vessel," after the area where the wreck had been discovered. The largely intact, reasonably well-preserved, 50-foot-long, open vessel was typical of the ships constructed locally for coastal trade around 1700, the approximate date of this wreck. The Brown's Ferry Vessel was, at the time, documented as the oldest vessel in existence known to have been built in North America. I studied it for well over an hour; it touched me on a personal level.

Cornelius Dougherty, an early ancestor of mine, had been living in the wilderness of what is now north Georgia at about that time with his Cherokee wife, and he owned a vessel much like this one. He used to transport his goods from the Savannah river to Charleston before the colony of Georgia was founded. A prosperous man many years later when Oglethorpe arrived to establish the colony of Georgia, Cornelius helped secure a peaceful arrangement with his in-laws, the Indians, for the settlement at Savannah. He made his ship available to transport supplies from Charleston to Savannah, in consideration of which the Trustees of the new colony granted him a tract of land along the Savannah River in the vicinity of what is now Augusta. I knew this from my father's genealogical research and from the colonial records, but seeing a vessel very like the one he had owned suddenly made it seem real to me.

Georgetown, S.C. to Awendaw Creek – Oysters for the Taking

My parents got married during the Great Depression. As a result, they lived frugally for their entire lives. They were also well-organized and determined to control every aspect of their lives, including disposal of their remains after death. Accordingly, they made arrangements, many years in advance, with a local funeral home in Savannah for the most inexpensive cremation, directing that their ashes be disposed of in "the most economical manner." They died within a few months of one another, and as I was settling their account with the manager of the funeral home, I wondered what "the most economical manner" had actually been. The manager was a contemporary of mine. He wasn't someone that I knew well, but we shared the bond of having grown up in Savannah when it was a relatively small place, before it became the tourist and retirement Mecca that it is now.

So I asked him, "What do you do with the ashes in a case like my folks'? My sister and I were both wondering."

He looked at me for a couple of beats, obviously making some assessment. "Just between us?"

"Sure," I said.

"You and your sister aren't sentimental."

I shook my head. "No, I reckon you could say that."

"Well," he said, clearly making a decision in the brief pause before he went on, "my folks retired to a little farm over in South Ca'lina, and I drive up there every weekend to check on 'em. They're a little younger than your folks, but you know how it is."

I nodded. "Mm-hmm."

"When I have ashes like that, I rip the plastic pouch open and hold it out the car window when I'm crossing the Santee River Bridge."

That made perfect sense to me and to my sister. We thought it was particularly fitting for my father, the avid fisherman. He knew that river well, and we had spent many happy hours fishing there for striped bass. My mother would have been less than happy, though. She had never liked boats and the water, barely tolerating the few times that my father had managed to persuade her to go out on the water with him.

The Santee River crosses the Waterway between Georgetown and Charleston, and even though I wasn't sentimental, I thought it would be nice to spend the night anchored in the river that had carried my folks on the last stage of their journey. We were late leaving Georgetown, not because anything was wrong, but because we had reached a part of the coast where tidal currents are a significant factor in navigation. Given the day's tides, by waiting for a favorable current to help carry us down Winyah Bay, we saved a few hours on the trip, leaving a bit later and arriving at the Santee River at about the same time as if we had fought the foul current, with less wear and tear on ourselves and the boat.

There was a cold front predicted for tomorrow, but by then we would be in well-protected waters on our approach to Charleston. We got underway at around 10:00 a.m. and had a fast ride down Winyah Bay to the Esterville-Minim Creek Canal, where the Waterway turns south again behind Cat Island. The sky had grown ominously dark for mid-afternoon. We had a moderate breeze behind us, helping the current push us along. When we made the 90-degree turn into the canal, our boat speed was no longer subtracted from the wind speed. What had seemed to be a mild breeze when blowing from behind us was revealed as a strong wind when it blew at a right angle to our course. As it howled in our rigging, we realized that the cold front was upon us, some 12 hours earlier than forecast.

We motored along the canal with the wind blowing directly across our path, and we realized that with the 20 to 25 knots of northwest wind, the Santee River, a few miles ahead, would not make a comfortable anchorage. At the point where we would cross, it was quite wide, mostly very shallow, and open to the northwest for several miles. We studied the charts, looking for an alternative spot where we would have a little more protection for the night. As we crossed the Santee, we found a serious wind chop on the river with steep two-to-three-foot waves rolling downstream. There were occasional breaking waves where the chop hit a shallow spot, and the air was filled with wind-driven spray. Indeed, it was not a place to spend a quiet night. I'm sure my mother was not happy with her final resting place that evening.

We decided instead to anchor in Bulls Bay, a part of the Cape Romaine national wildlife refuge. We followed the Waterway to its intersection with Awendaw Creek, which turns off to the south and runs a short distance to open into Bulls Bay. The word 'bay' doesn't conjure up an accurate picture of the setting that we found. Awendaw Creek took us into a wide, relatively deep pool of water surrounded by miles of marsh. Looking back the way we came, we could see the high ground with trees in the distance, and looking in the other direction we saw marsh grass dwindling to the horizon. We knew that there were innumerable small streams through the grass that emptied into the ocean some miles to the southeast, but none were obvious to us. We had a new appreciation for the term, 'wetlands.' As exposed as we were to the howling wind, we felt quite secure. The miles of marsh grass that surrounded us gave the wind no purchase on the water's surface, so there were no waves to mar the glass-like surface.

It was about an hour before low water, and the tidal range is about five or six feet along this segment of the coast. As we dropped the anchor close to the middle of the pool, I noticed that the exposed mud banks all around us were thick with oysters. I could also see signs, standing on posts, spaced every hundred yards or so along the mud banks. Busy setting the anchor, I assumed that they proclaimed some waterman's exclusive right to harvest the oysters, but they were too far away for me to read, even with the binoculars. As the anchor bit soundly into the mud bottom, I admired our surroundings for a few minutes. It was almost dusk, and we were the only boat around; we had not seen anyone else since Georgetown. Those signposts notwithstanding, I had a powerful craving for fresh oysters. Whoever had the rights to the beds surely wouldn't begrudge a weary traveler enough fresh oysters for supper.

I stepped back into the cockpit as Leslie shut down the diesel. "Want some oysters?" I asked her.

She looked up from the engine control panel. "What? Where?"

Leslie grew up in California's central valley. Her family's roots are deeply planted in the rich soil of Nebraska, where her ancestors homesteaded before the Civil War. She went to college in Nebraska and first encountered oysters when she moved to Houston for her first real job, about the time she met me. She quickly became fond of them, slurping them down in trendy oyster bars in Houston and New Orleans, where big, single specimens were shucked at the bar before your eyes for the price of a dollar apiece.

"Right here," I said. My own roots were planted just as deeply in the rich mud of the estuaries along the southeast coast, and my experience with oysters began when I was a child. They were ready-made snack food when the fish weren't biting.

"You serious?" she wanted to know.

"Let's launch the dinghy. You remember that oyster stew recipe?"

"I'm sure we have it in the recipe cards," she said, clearly humoring me as we dropped the dinghy and scrambled down into it.

I started rowing to the nearest mud bank, inhaling deeply, enjoying the salt-marsh tang in the air. I felt at home here.

"What do those signs say?"

"Can't read 'em yet," I replied.

"Where are the oysters? How do we get them?"

"You'll see. Just hang on." I pulled steadily at the oars.

"I can read the signs," she said. "They say 'South Carolina Public Shellfish Bed -- Recreational Harvesting Only.' I guess it's okay for us to take some oysters, but where are they?"

Knowing what the signs said took some of the excitement out of it, but I still wanted oysters, even if they were legal.

The dinghy ground to a halt as the water shoaled. We were sitting in a few inches of water. I stood and moved aft, reducing the draft at the bow; I used an oar to push us farther up onto the bank. Donning my work gloves and reaching over the side, I picked up clumps of shell and mud the size of basketballs and tossed them into the dinghy.

"What's that? You're getting mud in the dinghy," Leslie admonished me.

"Those 're your oysters," I said.

She looked dubious as I moved the dinghy a few feet to a fresh spot and continued my harvest. Leslie watched in silence. I kept working for a few more minutes, until I had about a half a bushel of the muddy lumps. There wasn't much more room in the dinghy, and the tide was coming in. I rowed us back to *Play Actor* as the sun set below the dark clouds of the cold front, casting a warm, rosy hue over the marsh.

I tied the dinghy alongside, and Leslie scrambled aboard the big boat. "You'd better use the wash-down hose on yourself. Want me to get it for you?"

"Not just yet. I need a rigging knife and a bowl. I'll clean up later."

She was back in a minute, handing me the knife and a stainless steel bowl. She sat on the side of *Play Actor*, watching with interest as I opened the knife and picked up one of the muddy clumps. I reached over the side of the dinghy and swished the clump vigorously through the clean seawater for a few seconds. Then I held it up for her inspection. She studied the accretion of small shells for a moment, touching the seaweed that bristled from it and watching the tiny crabs scurry around.

"They're so small," she remarked, "and all stuck together. And that's the littlest crab I've ever seen."

As I began to pry the clump of shells apart with the knife, I told her about how oyster stew aficionados always served one live oyster crab in each bowl of stew.

"Why?" she wanted to know.

"Proves that the stew wasn't overcooked. If you get it hot enough to kill the crab, it ruins the oysters."

"So do you eat the crab?"

"Sure," I said, popping one in my mouth.

Leslie's not squeamish about food. When she accompanied me on business trips to Asia, she was often treated to some unusual delicacies, and she had acquired a taste for some things that most westerners found odd; fish eyes were just one example.

"I'll try it." She reached out a hand, and I gave her a crab.

"It didn't have much taste," she remarked.

"Try this," I said, offering her the first, small oyster.

She took the shell from me and carefully slurped the morsel into her mouth, closing her eyes and moaning with delight at the sudden, salty burst of flavor.

"I never had an oyster that tasted like that," she said, reaching for the one I had just shelled.

I smiled at her pleasure and concentrated on shucking oysters, reaching behind me to drop them in the bowl as I made a mental note to pick up an oyster knife in Charleston. The rigging knife was doing the job, but the sharp edge was chipping the shells. I had noticed a few flakes of shell in the oyster I had just sampled. As I savored the taste, I remembered why I didn't bother to eat raw oysters very often. After growing up eating them like this, the ones in restaurants just had no flavor. Perhaps it was the obsession for only serving big oysters, or maybe it was because they weren't as fresh. Before I picked up another clump of muddy oysters, I reached behind me for the bowl to see what progress I had made. I was shocked that it was empty. I looked up to see Leslie, eyes closed, licking her lips, a decidedly cat-like expression on her face.

"Hey, you," I said. "Go below and get that recipe, before you eat all the oysters. It's too late to get more tonight."

She did find the recipe, although we had to substitute soy milk laden with butter for the specified milk and heavy cream, as that was all we had in our larder. The stew didn't suffer for it, and the little crabs were still alive, just slightly tinged with red from the heat of cooking. Life was never better.

Awendaw Creek to Charleston, S.C.

We left Awendaw Creek early; we were eager to get to Charleston. We had enjoyed some fine times there over the years, but we had never visited by boat before and Charleston, like Annapolis, had the reputation of turning her best face to the sea. We had just finished lunch underway when we entered Charleston Harbor, where the natives say the Ashley River and the Cooper River join to form the Atlantic Ocean. Although that's said with at least a small trace of humor, the confluence of the Ashley and the Cooper does form an impressive harbor. As we followed the marked channel, we left the entrance from the deep, well marked inlet on our port side, noticing that the seawater coming in with the rising tide was a clear, green color compared to the somewhat darker, brown water of the last several miles in the Waterway. It was a sunny, warm, beautiful day, and Leslie stood on the foredeck taking in the view as she helped me spot the next channel marker. All of a sudden, she shrieked and pointed toward the intersection with the channel from the inlet on the port side.

Momentarily worried, I was reaching for the throttle to slow us down when she yelled again, this time quite clearly. "Porpoises!"

I looked in the direction she was pointing just in time to see a couple of big ones leap clear of the water, streaking directly toward us when they slipped back beneath the surface. Soon, a large school of them, perhaps 25 or 30, swam alongside the boat. It has always charmed me when these creatures do this. It was obvious that they knew we were there, watching them as they went through a routine of the same stunts that their captive cousins perform for the pleasure of the crowds in dolphin shows. These were not trained, but they were clearly performing. Leslie was entranced, yelling encouragement as they leapt and swirled a few feet from her. She applauded loudly, and they appeared to respond with ever more intricate tricks. After 15 or 20 minutes, Leslie and the porpoises were tired, and the porpoises disappeared as quickly as they had come.

Leslie joined me in the cockpit to finish our morning thermos of coffee as we worked our way through the harbor past the Battery and into the mouth of the Ashley River. We had reservations for two weeks at Charleston's City Marina. My sister would drive up from Savannah in a couple of days to spend some time showing us around the town, familiar to her from long association. Before he died a few years earlier, she and her husband had lived in Walterboro, a small town not far from Charleston, where they owned a hardware store. He had attended the Citadel, officially the Military College of South Carolina, and was from an old Charleston-area family, although he had grown up in Savannah. He had a seemingly infinite number of relatives in the area, with most of whom my sister still kept in touch. She planned to spend a few days showing us around so that we would be competent tour guides ourselves when Leslie's parents arrived later in the week for their Thanksgiving visit.

Charleston marked the approximate midpoint of our route down the Waterway, and we were ready for a break from our routine. Showers at the marina with unlimited hot water sounded sinfully attractive after weeks of restricted water use. Since we were using the engine every day, we had been enjoying hot showers; our water heater uses waste heat from the engine. Hot showers were one thing, but we were still trying to become accustomed to rationing water. We carry about 100 gallons of fresh water, which sounds like a lot until you realize that the average two-person household uses some 300 to 500 gallons per day, not including watering lawns. We had managed by this time to get our own use down to about three gallons per day, including drinking, bathing, cooking, and washing dishes, but it was a constant struggle. No wonder the idea of showering under a continuous flow of hot water sounded good to us.

And we wouldn't have to worry about electricity, either. We could use all the electricity we wanted: lights, heat, water heater – we wouldn't have to light the diesel-fueled heater if it got cold during our visit. The diesel heater, which resembled an ultramodern potbellied stove, put out a lot of heat, but the electric heaters were much better for maintaining an even temperature in our cabin. We were looking forward to a life of luxury for a couple of weeks. We actually had not been conscious of missing these things until we saw the prospect of plenty on the horizon.

We tied *Play Actor* to the dock and did the marina paperwork. Then we returned to the boat to organize our thoughts. Aside from enjoying some unaccustomed luxuries, there were some boat improvements that we wanted to accomplish while we had easy access to marine supplies. I had mentioned electricity. One of our projects was to buy and install a battery monitor. All our electricity aboard comes from our house battery bank, which must be recharged periodically. We had installed solar panels and a wind turbine before we moved aboard, and those provided a substantial percentage of the energy required to keep the batteries up. Any shortfall, and there was always some, was made up by running the diesel, which had a powerful alternator. It was like the alternator on a car, but larger. By running the diesel, we could fully charge the batteries in about four hours. With no charge coming from the wind or the sun, our batteries alone would provide about two days worth of our electrical needs.

One of life's persistent questions, along with, "How much water is left in the tanks," and "How much diesel fuel do we have left," had become, "When do we need to charge the batteries?" Waiting until they were dead would permanently damage them. Charging them unnecessarily was also harmful to them, as well as being inefficient, not to mention being a major nuisance. The diesel is noisy and the vibration is fatiguing. It's almost in our living room, remember, so we didn't want to run it more than we had to, just to generate electricity. One of our planned improvements in Charleston was the addition of a new instrument, an amp-hour meter, which would monitor our electrical usage so that we would have a definitive answer to at least that one question about when to charge the batteries. I had ordered one of these, to be shipped to a local marine supply store.

We realized by the time we reached Charleston that we were managing these tradeoffs pretty well. Water and electricity problems, coupled with persistent boat maintenance headaches, were taking their toll among the other new cruisers we had met. It's one thing to read about these inconveniences in the comfort of your home ashore, but to live with them constantly for months is a different thing. By the time we reached Charleston, we had run into more than one couple who vowed to sell their boat when they got to Florida and go "home." The fact that we felt sadness at their disappointment when we heard people say things like that was indicative of our level of adjustment to the demands of our new life.

****

We enjoyed our two weeks in Charleston. It was great fun having my sister show us the sights and fill us in on local lore, as well as introducing us to some of her favorite restaurants. By the time Leslie's folks arrived for their week's visit, we were old Charleston hands. Compared to the tour guide from Ohio who drove the horse-drawn carriage for the tour that the four of us took of the historic district, we were practically locals.

Leslie's parents are both classical musicians. They founded and ran a small opera company for many years, and thus had a finely tuned appreciation for Charleston's historic association with the arts. We all especially enjoyed visiting the Dock Street Theatre, which was the first building in North America designed and constructed for theatrical performances.

It was at the Dock Street Theatre that my ancestor Dennis Ryan performed in May of 1785. Following the performance, the Columbian Herald and Patriotic Courier of North America (a local newspaper in 18th-century Charleston – the title says a lot about how the city perceived its own importance, even back then) reported in the shipping news for May 7, 1785: "Dennis Ryan and his American Company of Comedians sailed today for Baltimore aboard the schooner, *Play Actor*, after having been denied permission to play Savannah."

Dennis owned the company and the schooner; Baltimore was his home. Some narrow minded folks have always viewed theatrical performance as injurious to the public morals; rabid conservatism is nothing new in this country's political makeup. Some 40 years ago, I donated Dennis Ryan's business records to the Maryland Historical Society. The files included a number of letters to state governors along the East Coast seeking permission to perform; clearly, permission wasn't always forthcoming. The owner of the current *Play Actor* learned from this; I act without asking for permission and beg forgiveness if necessary.

After spending a week observing life aboard the modern *Play Actor,* Leslie's folks were a bit less dubious about their daughter's choice to run away to sea. We had cooked a nice Thanksgiving dinner aboard for them, and they had made note of the fact that while they were seeing Charleston as short-term visitors, we were living at home and enjoying the city for as long as we chose to stay. This was a relief to me, as much earlier in our relationship her mother's initial reaction to our goal of sailing away had been, "Not with my daughter you don't." She had said it in a joking tone, but her anxiety had been visible just the same. She was much less worried after seeing how well this life suited her only daughter.

In our spare time, we had completed our list of boat projects and managed to stock up on groceries yet again. We were only a few days from Savannah, and before we got there, we had planned stops in Beaufort, South Carolina, (That's pronounced Bū-faht, not to be confused with Beaufort (Bō-fert), North Carolina.) and Bluffton, South Carolina, where we would spend a few days visiting with my sister's husband's cousin, who lived on the May River.

Access to grocery shopping wouldn't be a problem for the next couple of weeks, but we were getting anxious to move on, as the weather was getting chilly. We wanted to see Beaufort and it was at the right distance for an overnight pause anyway. Bluffton and Savannah were stops to visit with family; we didn't want to have to spend our time there buying groceries. Besides, we had discovered a great gourmet grocery store within walking distance of downtown, the best we had found since Annapolis, and it was easy to get to.

As our two weeks in Charleston drew to a close, we added this to our list of places to which we would return for a longer, less structured stay. Aside from its beauty and charm, one of the things we liked best about Charleston was that it was so easy to get around on foot. Most of the places we wanted to visit were within a reasonable walk from the marina.

Charleston, S.C. to Bluffton, S.C.

An early morning departure from Charleston gave us a favorable current through Wapoo Creek from the Ashley River to the Stono River. Although Wappoo Creek is only about three miles long, the current that rips through it as the tides equalize between the two rivers can approach the speed of a slow boat. Having a favorable current is the difference between spending a few minutes in transit or slogging along for the better part of the morning.

We were a bit surprised at how many southbound cruising boats were traveling with us. We had expected that our two-week hiatus in Charleston would put us well behind the crowd, but it seems that a lot of people left their boats somewhere in the vicinity of Charleston and went home to spend the holiday with family.

Beaufort, the next place where we plan to stop for longer than a night, is around 70 miles down the Waterway. That was farther than we wanted to travel in a day; pushing on to Beaufort would have meant arriving well after dark. There's a lot of beautiful country between Charleston and Beaufort if your taste, like ours, runs to pristine marshlands. When we had covered about half the distance to Beaufort, we began to look for an attractive anchorage.

As we entered the Ashepoo River, we found ourselves admiring the high bluff on the north bank. The shoreline was heavily wooded, with just a couple of small houses visible. The soil of the bluff, a mixture of sand and clay, crumbled in a sheer drop of 30 feet or more. At the foot of the bluff there was a shingle of muddy beach with a few dead trees that had tumbled from the higher ground at some point, the soil having eroded from around their roots. It seemed to be a quiet spot, not at all out of our way, and it was mid-afternoon. We dropped the anchor a hundred yards from the beach and spent the afternoon relaxing until dinner time.

We only saw one or two boats pass during the afternoon; most of the crowd from Charleston continued south after we stopped. Had we not been timing our arrival in Bluffton to meet my sister, we might have gone a little farther ourselves, but this stop would put us in Beaufort late tomorrow morning. We could spend the afternoon sightseeing among the fine antebellum houses there and still have a comfortably short trip on to Bluffton the following day.

The Waterway from Beaufort south was familiar territory for me. My father and I had spent countless hours fishing these waters when I was growing up. While the waters were familiar, I was struck by how heavily most of the shoreline had been developed in the last 30 to 40 years. What had been woodlands back then now sported condos and gated, golf-course communities. We were getting close to Hilton Head, ground zero for the explosion of golfing communities and resorts. The mouth of the May River, which leads to Bluffton, opens to the west as the Waterway passes the midpoint of Hilton Head's western shore.

The last time I passed this way by boat, the development of Hilton Head had barely begun; there wasn't much there but an attractive beach where a few local people had built basic, concrete-block beach houses. One friend of my father's had such a house. We would occasionally tie the boat up to a ramshackle dock at a general store, and my father would borrow the phone at the store to call his friend, who would come down to the dock and visit, perhaps to be given a mess of fresh fish, if we'd had a good day. I remember once being driven across Hilton Head to the beach in a war surplus Jeep, along a treacherous dirt road. As we took in the wall-to-wall houses and condos along the Waterway, I couldn't begin to figure out where that old dock would have been, and certainly, no dirt roads could have survived on the island.

As we turned off into the May River, the surroundings looked much more familiar to me. We throttled back for a few minutes to watch a bald eagle circling, apparently looking for fish. When the eagle moved on without catching anything, we resumed our trip up the river. The entrance to the river is wide and deep, although it's necessary to watch the channel markers once well inside the mouth. The north shore of the May had a few houses in evidence; the south shore was mostly marshy, with a few wooded hummocks of high ground. As we followed the channel around the first bend, we held our breath, eyes glued to the depth sounder. This spot has always shoaled, and although I had been through it many times years ago, I had never carried six feet of draft with any of those other boats. As the water got very shallow, we felt ourselves bump the mud bottom a couple of times, but we kept the faith. The tide was rising; if we got stuck it would only be for a little while. Once we were through the shallow spot, our cell phone rang.

When I gave the helm to Leslie and answered the phone, my sister said, "We see you! John just went down to the dock; he's going to hang a big yellow flag so you'll know which dock is his."

A flicker of yellow caught my eye as we said goodbye and disconnected. I reached for the binoculars and soon saw a replica of the old Gadsden flag with its yellow field and rattlesnake poised to strike. As the breeze stretched it out, the motto "Don't tread on me!" was clear. After being steeped in colonial maritime history for most of our journey, we were advancing to the early days of the Republic; John was a proud veteran of World War II, although despite the flag, he had served in the Army Air Corps rather than the Navy or the Marine Corps. The flag, however, did suit his personality. We were soon tied securely to his floating dock. As we scrambled up the steep gangway to the bluff where the house stood, I turned to look back toward the river. I noticed that we were at eye level with the top of *Play Actor's* 57-foot mast.

"Never realized how high your bluff was, John," I remarked. "Guess you don't worry about flooding from the storm surge."

"Naw," he replied, eyeing the crumbling edge of the clay and sand precipice. "But I lose a few feet every year. Figure I'll be gone before the house falls in, though. Hope so, anyhow."

We had a pleasant visit of a couple days with John and his wife and my sister and one of her childhood friends, a constant companion for her entire life. John, as I mentioned earlier, was a cousin of my sister's husband, and an old friend of my father's, as well. He was a fascinating character, and I always enjoyed his company. He had grown up as the son of a subsistence farmer on the remains of one of his family's plantations. After the war, he had gotten a degree in English Literature thanks to the G.I. Bill, and then he had gone to work as a boiler tender at the power company in nearby Savannah. Shortly after that, he and his wife had bought the modest house where we stood. It had been out in the back of beyond, then; now they were besieged by developers offering them a literal fortune for the few acres of unspoiled waterfront upon which it stood. They weren't interested; they had lived a life of simple contentment for over 50 years in that spot, and they had no other ambition. John had inherited the plantation not far away, but at the same time, a cousin of his had been granted a life estate in the property, so other than making him legally responsible for the taxes on the hundreds of acres, John's inheritance didn't mean much.

John's ancestors had once owned most of that part of South Carolina, including the land where all the gated communities now stand, and in his old age, his biggest worry was whether his Social Security payments would keep pace with the escalating property taxes on his little house.

I told him that I wanted to take Leslie to Hilton Head while we were in the area.

"Why? When did you last see it?" he asked.

"Early 60s, and she's never been there," I replied.

"Well, I reckon you ought to go see it, then. But when you cross that bridge you'll see it's not part of South Ca'lina anymore. Nothin' there but Yankees and their gated communities. Used to be, they put gates up to keep the stock in. Now, they put 'em up to keep folks like you 'n' me out, Bud."

John was a consummate outdoorsman, having spent his life hunting and fishing. It always amused my father that John would shoot deer whenever the spirit moved him. He kept a freezer full of venison. When asked about hunting season and hunting licenses, he would say that was for the newcomers. He maintained that King Charles had granted his family the right to hunt the King's deer in perpetuity when they had settled in the area. Although a veteran and an all-American patriot, he still took that hereditary privilege to heart.

On our second morning there, John and his wife fed us a hearty breakfast of eggs, grits, biscuits, and venison sausage -- from the King's deer, of course. Thus fortified against the bitter cold that had settled in the low country overnight, we set out for Savannah with my sister and her friend aboard *Play Actor*. It was a short, scenic trip. My sister and her friend were real troopers, eschewing the warm cabin below in favor of riding on deck with us. They both wanted to see the scenery, and deemed the dramatic vistas of woodland and marsh well worth the minor discomfort of the chilly, late-fall day.

Bluffton, S.C. to Thunderbolt, Ga., and on to Killkenny Creek

We spent a night at one of the marinas in Thunderbolt, Georgia, a small place squeezed between Savannah and the Wilmington River, which was the natural route the Waterway took through this area. We had dinner ashore in one of the old places at Thunderbolt that served nothing but fresh, local seafood, prepared simply and presented on paper plates at tables covered with newspaper. In the center of each table was a two-foot-square hole, underneath which was a trash can. The standard fare in the place had been steamed shrimp or crabs for as long as I could remember, and you simply pushed the piles of shells into the hole as they got in your way. The same family had always run the little place, and unlike most of the newer spots along the waterfront with the lines outside their doors, this one served only tea and soft drinks with their fried or steamed seafood. "No good comes of serving alcohol," the waitress said, when I remarked that they still adhered to that long-standing policy. "Folks come here to eat. Them as wants to drink, there's plenty of other places."

After dinner, we said goodbye to my sister and her friend. They had left a car at Thunderbolt, and we were planning to leave early the next morning. Savannah was a place where Leslie and I had spent a lot of time in recent years, visiting with my folks in their declining years, and most of the sights were best seen from downtown anyway. Downtown Savannah isn't readily accessible from the Waterway; although it's a thriving commercial seaport, Savannah's waterfront is several miles up the Savannah River from where the Waterway crosses the river's ship channel. There were limited facilities for pleasure boats along the waterfront downtown, and the trip up the river wasn't attractive.

Alone again, we settled down in our snug cabin for the evening, and our conversation turned to replaying the last couple of days with John and his wife. All married couples have patterns of conversation that repeat; perhaps the longer they're married, the more often they're repeated. John's wife was a sociable lady, always chipper and outgoing. Anytime we were around them for a while, we would eventually hear her say to John, "Let's go somewhere, John. We aren't getting any younger."

Shortly after his retirement, they had done some traveling, including a pilgrimage to Ireland, to see where their ancestors had come from; they weren't untraveled people. As John got older, though, he became more of a homebody as she grew more restless. His gruff reply to her frequent conversational gambit was invariably, "I *am* somewhere!"

We laughed about that as we followed the Wilmington River to the next turning of the Waterway, and I recounted for Leslie my conversation with John the night before we left Bluffton. We were standing in front of the house while the ladies bustled about the kitchen fixing dinner. As the setting sun bathed the endless miles of marshland across the May River in a warm, red-orange glow, it lent a crimson hue to the fluffy, white clouds. When the dramatic colors reached their peak, John said, in a soft tone, almost to himself, it seemed, "There's no more beautiful place on earth than here; why would a man go anywhere else, if he didn't have to?"

We envied John his contentment, and hoped that we would find our own when we were his age.

****

The miles slipped easily under our keel, and soon we were passing Isle of Hope, another very old, waterfront suburb of Savannah. It had taken us the better part of three hours; I mentioned to Leslie that the last time I remembered making the trip, I had done it in 20 minutes on water-skis. She looked at me for a minute. "I hope it was warmer," she finally said, shivering as she poured coffee from our thermos.

"A little," I said, remembering when Barbee's Pavilion had been the most prominent feature along Isle of Hope's shoreline. When I had been in high school, it had been a popular venue for dances and other forms of entertainment, but it had been gone for a long time. With the exception of the loss of the pavilion and the addition of a fairly modern looking marina, the waterfront didn't appear much different. It was an attractive stretch of shoreline, with a number of beautiful older houses overlooking the water. They were separated from the bluff by the road that wound along in the shade of the old oaks, but the road was invisible from the water.

Within an hour, we were crossing Moon River, made famous by the song of the same name. It had been called Back River until the popularity of the song by Johnny Mercer, one of Savannah's native sons, prompted the state to officially rename the river. When the tide is high, it's much as described in the song, but it was near low water when we passed, and the nine-foot tidal drop exposed the sandbars and mud flats that make the river a navigational challenge to all but small boats.

As we proceeded, we frequently heard other southbound sailboats calling one of the towing services for assistance. Although the Waterway channel is well-marked, it's narrow and winding, and the scenic shoreline provides ample distractions. Especially at low tide, a moment's inattention will result in running solidly aground. Aside from the embarrassment, this rarely causes damage; the bottom is relatively soft, and the rising tide will refloat most boats, albeit with a delay of six to eight hours. Most people, of course, don't want to wait. We passed one large sailboat which was completely high and dry, lying on its side in the mud, a hundred yards from the water. Gentle waves lapped at the edge of the mud, taunting the hapless occupants of the boat. A man and a woman sat disconsolately on the high side of the boat, some eight to ten feet in the air, watching the rest of us go by.

"How did he get there?" Leslie wondered, aloud.

"Ran aground at high tide," I responded. That's a whole different situation from running aground at low tide. With the speed at which the water level drops, a boat that runs aground at high tide is unlikely to get free until the next high tide, if then. Because the level of the tides changes with the phase of the moon, it's possible that the next high tide won't be as high as the one that left the boat stranded. Of course, you can wait for the lunar cycle to come around again, but that takes more days than most people are willing to wait. The other problem that comes from a grounding like the one we just passed is that the rising tide may flood the boat, depending on how far it's inclined from the horizontal. If the boat is grounded on a steeply sloped mud bank and the deck is at or past 90 degrees to the horizontal, this is a serious threat, although that doesn't happen often.

In my youth, I stood with the mud from many of these hazards oozing between the toes of my bare feet, fishing as the incoming tide brought the bounty of the sea to me. I knew well the bank that had trapped the hapless cruiser we just passed.

"How will he get off?" Leslie asked.

"Well, there's only around three feet of water over that mud bank at high tide, so it'll be a challenge. He must have been trying to sail when he hit it, with the boat heeled over; if he had been upright, he couldn't have gotten so far up on the bank." If a sailboat draws five feet of water when it's upright, it might only draw three feet when tipped to the side under full sail. "They'll have to wait for high water – around 10:00 p.m. tonight, I think – and then they'll need help from one of those towboats."

"Glad it's not us," Leslie remarked.

"Me, too."

We spent the afternoon traversing waters that evoked one childhood memory after another; fortunately, my wife is a patient person and pretended to find my ramblings interesting. A lot of our fellow cruisers had warned us that the Waterway through Georgia was the worst part of the trip. They were usually the self-proclaimed experts, the ones who had made the trip before, and they didn't realize they were talking about the area that I will always consider home.

"It's shallow," they complained.

There's a lot of shallow water in the marshlands. There's also plenty of deep, navigable water for those who take the trouble to look at their navigation charts.

"It's boring; there's nothing to see there, and with a foul current and the winding rivers, it takes forever," they told us.

It's true that there are miles and miles of winding rivers. You can see the mast of a boat half a mile away across the marsh and know that it's several miles away, given the twists and turns of the winding channel through the marsh. It would have been much faster to drive to Florida on the interstate, or to go out into the ocean at Charleston and sail for 24 hours to the St. Mary's inlet on the Florida-Georgia state line. Of course, most of the self-proclaimed experts thought that sailing at night was dangerous and that sailing in the ocean was even more dangerous. If you don't time your travel on this part of the Waterway to take into account the tides, the currents can be a problem. To me, the marshlands, with their varied and abundant wildlife, are a place of singular beauty. From birds to beaver, otters to osprey, there's some wonderful creature waiting just around the next bend.

"It's lonely and dangerous," one couple told us. "We had to anchor all by ourselves, one night, and just at dark, this decrepit old shrimp boat came up and anchored."

"Did you take the dinghy over to see if they had fresh shrimp?" I asked, having failed to connect the shrimp boat to the 'dangerous' comment.

"No! Those people are scary. They're not like us. Didn't you see Deliverance? It was about Georgia, you know."

The world can be a hazardous place for some people; I suppose their expectations color a lot of their encounters with folks who are 'not like us.' We cherished anchorages where we were the only boat, and one of the best parts of the Waterway through Georgia is that there are so many beautiful, secluded places to anchor.

We turned off the Waterway into Kilkenny Creek just before sunset; only the entrance to the creek is shown on the strip chart of the Waterway which most folks use, but it's navigable for a long way past the edge of the chart. I knew that 35 years earlier there had been a little fishing camp and marina well up the creek, but we didn't go that far. We found a deep, wide spot at a bend, half-surrounded by marsh grass, and dropped our anchor as the sun was setting. As we sat in the cockpit taking in our surroundings in the rapidly fading light, a shrimp boat came by. The man at the helm offered a friendly wave, but he didn't anchor. I was a little disappointed; one of those childhood memories was of a time when a friend and I had approached a shrimp boat at anchor in a spot like this.

Two rough looking men had been hard at work on the aft deck, squaring away their gear after a hard day's work. One of them looked up as we drew alongside.

"Hey, boys. Can I hep you fellers?" he asked.

We were out of bait. "Sell us a few shrimp for bait?"

"Sure. Gimme ya bucket."

I passed a bucket up to him as my companion held onto the battered rail of the little trawler. We watched as the man set the bucket on deck and picked up a shovel. He dipped the shovel into the hold and dumped a shovelful of shrimp and ice into the bucket. He hefted the bucket, then set it back down and added another shovelful. Satisfied, he handed me the brim-full bucket.

"That do ye?" he asked.

"Yessir. How much I owe you?"

"Shovelful a shrimp ain't nothin'. It's gettin' late, boy. Why don't you fergit fishin' today an' take them shrimp on home? Eat 'em fer supper while they fresh. You don't owe me nothin' but a thank you and good evenin'."

"Yessir. Thank you, sir, and good evenin'." He waved as he watched us race for home with enough shrimp for several days of good eating. That was one of the best days of fishing I ever had, and we didn't even catch anything.

I had a different perspective on shrimpers than our expert cruising acquaintances. I could still taste those shrimp, but Leslie and I made do with peanut butter and jelly sandwiches that night in Kilkenny Creek. After endless family feasts for the last couple of weeks, neither of us had much appetite.

Kilkenny Creek to the Crescent River

Our anchorage was peaceful last night; there was the sound of the breeze softly kissing the marsh grass, and the occasional squawk of some bird hunting in the moonlight. We slept soundly, and we were awakened by the gentle gray light of dawn coming through the portholes. I crawled out from under our down comforter and put a pot of espresso on the stove. As the fragrant liquid began to stream into the stainless steel pitcher, Leslie joined me in the galley, savoring the warmth from the stove as she made our breakfast. We were soon back on the Waterway, moving south all by ourselves, as there were no natural gathering points for the other boats around here.

As the sun rose higher, we shed our down jackets, and soon, our sweaters. With no wind, it was a warm day; quite a change from the bone-chilling cold of the last couple of days. People retire to this part of the country for the mild winters, but near-freezing temperatures in the damp air out on the water feel much colder than they feel ashore. By mid-morning, we had finished our thermos of coffee and were wearing T-shirts and our blue jeans.

When were crossing St. Catherine's Sound, near its wide opening to the sea, a school of porpoises appeared, cavorting under our bowsprit for 15 or 20 minutes. Leslie was enthralled by them; this was only her second close encounter with the amazing creatures. She spent the time out on the bowsprit, yelling and clapping to encourage them as they cavorted just below her feet. We have read that they respond to noise from people on boats. We don't have any definitive evidence to support that theory, but watching them leap and twirl in mid-air as Leslie cheered them on made it easy for me to believe that they knew their performance had an appreciative audience.

Shortly after the dolphin show, Leslie made sandwiches for lunch, which we ate as we watched the endless vista of marshland. We were passing the inland side of St. Catherine's Island, which had been a private estate when I was growing up. Now it was a nature preserve, still closed to public access. I had spent a lot of time fishing around here, and we considered finding a spot to anchor for the night, but it was still a bit too early to stop.

We talked about how much farther we should go, deciding that stopping sooner rather than later would suit us. We had made good progress, having covered over 600 miles since we left Norfolk, Virginia, about six weeks ago. As we realized that, it struck us that we were averaging 100 miles per week. I recalled road trips across the southwest U.S. when I had been stationed at Fort Bliss, Texas, 30 years earlier, when I drove 600 miles in six hours. The contrast between the desert of the southwest and the marshlands where we were moving at a fraction of that pace was as stark as the contrast in speed.

Even though my reminiscing made us realize that we could have walked from Norfolk in six weeks it had taken us to get here, we weren't in a hurry. We were well over halfway to Miami, where we would leave the U.S. to sail to the Bahamas. Our daughter was joining us for the week between Christmas and New Year's Day in Melbourne, Florida, a little over 200 miles to the south of our present position. We had plenty of time to get there by Christmas and no need to arrive early.

We were about 65 miles from the St. Mary's River Inlet where we would leave Georgia and enter Florida. We planned to stop for a day or two and visit the Cumberland Island National Seashore, immediately north of the state line. Looking at the chart, we decided to spend two days covering that distance. We left the Waterway a few miles farther south to anchor in the Crescent River, just a mile or so from where it intersected the Waterway.

It was mid-afternoon by the time we anchored, and still pleasantly warm. We sat in the cockpit to read, distracted periodically by a great blue heron that was fishing in the shallows. At a distance, it was hard to realize how big those birds are, but I had come up into the cockpit early one morning a year or two ago and surprised one. It was standing on one of the seats, peering intently into the water alongside the boat, when I opened the companionway doors. We scared one another witless, that bird and I. With a loud, characteristic squawk, it spread its wings and beat the air furiously, narrowly missing my head in its panicked departure. It stood nearly four feet tall. They look spindly, until they spread those big wings; that one had a wing span that was easily four feet.

At a casual glance, the tall, slender birds look ungainly, but watching one stalk fish in a few inches of water reveals how graceful they truly are. Their movement is so slow and fluid that they appear motionless, head cocked to one side, an eye on the prey. If you blink, you miss the strike; it's a split-second blur. One second the bird is frozen, intent. The next, the long neck is whipping the head violently from side to side, a fish clutched in the long, sharp beak. After just a few shakes, the fish is too dazed to struggle, and the bird flips it with practiced ease so that the fish slides head-first down the inside of that long, impossibly thin neck. Once the bulge in its throat disappears into the bird's body, it resumes the hunt, looking for the next fish.

The heron stood out for us in the fading light, silhouetted against a small, low island rising out of the marsh. The dry ground was covered with brush and a few small trees. A loud, crashing sound in the undergrowth startled the heron and caught our attention as well. We watched with the heron as the bushes shook and their branches rattled, until a wild boar appeared, rooting in the soft soil where the little island rose from the marsh. The boar was a massive, shaggy, nightmarish creature; I shivered, remembering a few close encounters with them in the Florida swamps at night when I used to escape college for a weekend of bass fishing.

This was Leslie's first view of a wild boar, lending new meaning to the story John had told us a few days ago about one that he had killed. As he talked, Leslie had been examining the yellowed, five-inch-long curved tusk that John had kept as a trophy after it slashed his trouser leg. Boar hunting as it had been practiced in that part of the low country in John's youth had been a macho sport. One person in the hunting party would stand his ground, a heavy caliber pistol in hand, while his friends drove the boar toward the person with the pistol. When the boar was sufficiently provoked to charge, the hunter would shoot it in the head at point-blank range, stepping backward smartly as the 700 pound carcass slid to a stop within arm's reach. The consequences of missing that one shot didn't bear thinking about.

We went to bed early, tired from a day in the warm fresh air. It was warm enough that evening to sleep with the boat open;

we enjoyed the light breeze wafting through the cabin as we snuggled under the duvet.

St. Simon's Island to Cumberland Island

We spent the next night in the Frederica River where it passes west of St. Simon's Island on our way to Cumberland Island. We were anchored right off the Fort Frederica National Monument, which we had visited with the children, some 12 years previously, when they were indeed still children. As we sat in the cockpit watching the crowds of tourists walking around the site, Leslie asked, "When we were up there with Ryan and Dede, did you think we'd ever actually have *Play Actor* anchored out here in the river?"

After a minute's thought, I said, "I guess that I hoped we would, but it seemed far-fetched, back then."

She smiled and nodded.

There was another boat anchored off the Fort; it had appeared to be unoccupied when we arrived. We had noticed a dinghy, bobbing gently at the Park Service dock. A flash of motion caught our attention from the dock, and we glanced over to see a couple standing on the dock, looking down at the dinghy, now resting in the mud some 20 feet from the water. The bow of the dinghy was held a foot or two up in the air by the taut line that tied it to the dock. If you've never experienced an eight foot tidal range, it's hard to visualize what will happen if you tie your dinghy off on a short line at high tide. Most of the East Coast of the U.S. doesn't have even close to that kind of tidal range, so it surprises a lot of otherwise experienced boaters when they visit coastal Georgia. There's a relatively short stretch of the coastline that has that kind of range; it diminishes to half that just into South Carolina or Florida.

Of course, even if our hapless neighbors had left plenty of slack in their dinghy painter, the dinghy might still have ended up in the mud. Or, if it had stayed afloat, it would have been a long way from the dock, accessible only by climbing down and slogging through mud in which you might sink to your knees. They looked out at us, sitting in our cockpit, afloat in 20 feet of water, and no more than 50 yards away. I waved, and the man waved back. He cupped his hands around his mouth.

"What time is high water?" he asked.

"About 10:00 p.m.," I answered.

He shrugged and conferred with his wife for a minute. She shrugged as well, and then they both sat down on the dock and removed their shoes and socks, rolling up their blue jeans to their knees. The man untied the line and lowered the dinghy into the soft, black, mud. Then he sat on the edge of the dock, sliding forward until his feet were close to the mud. Giving himself a final push, he landed with a plop, settling into the mud until it almost reached his knees as his arms windmilled for balance. He turned around and reached up to help his wife down, sinking another few inches as he took her weight. Soon, the two of them were lifting and dragging their dinghy, a heavy-looking rigid inflatable with a sizable outboard. They each slipped and fell a few times, rising like some prehistoric creatures from the sticky, smelly, black ooze. They finally got the dinghy to the water and got it launched, holding on to it for balance as they tried to wash the worst of the mud from themselves and their clothes. Although it was a relatively warm afternoon, they were surely badly chilled by the time they got back to their boat.

"How could they have avoided that?" Leslie asked, her voice tinged with worry.

"Well, around here, if there's not a floating dock, then you time your visit to the tide; tie up and go ashore a few hours before high tide and leave within a few hours after. Or do what they did. Sometimes, you can find a sandy spot to beach the dinghy. That's not quite as messy, but you'll still have to drag it back to the water and get your feet wet."

She shook her head, clearly not interested in any excursions ashore that involved what we had just witnessed.

The next morning, we followed the Frederica River south. It paralleled the Waterway and had once been the Waterway channel, but at some point, the Corps of Engineers had decided that keeping the other, parallel watercourse dredged would be easier. At the south end of the river, we found just enough water at half-tide to allow us to rejoin the slightly deeper Waterway channel. If the tide had been lower, we would have had to wait in order to get out of the Frederica. Past the Fort, the Frederica River had taken us by some beautiful riverfront homes, set back in the shade of old oaks along the high bluff. It was pretty enough that it would have been worth the wait.

Soon, we were across St. Simon's Sound and the ship channel that provides access to the Port of Brunswick for ocean-going vessels. We tucked in behind Jekyll Island, and after a few miles, we turned into Jekyll Creek, which passes a number of historic homes on the Island. Jekyll was the private retreat of a number of wealthy families who belonged to the Jekyll Island Club from the late 1800s until the tax burden became so heavy that they turned it over to the state in the 1960s. The Jekyll Island Club's clubhouse, once the dining hall where the members took all their meals, still stands.

The Jekyll Island "cottages" of the 19th century's elite families rival the ones found along the New England shore, with the advantage of offering temperate weather in the winter months. The clubhouse itself, with a few elegant suites above the dining hall, has been a resort hotel for many years.

During that same trip with the children when we visited Fort Frederica, we stayed in the suite on the top floor of the Jekyll Island Club. Our sitting room had featured a spiral staircase leading up to a cupola, complete with an antique brass telescope. We had all enjoyed looking out over the marshes from up there. The suite itself was on the National Register of historic places and was part of several organized tours. As the bellman had shown us to our room, a large group with a tour guide was just leaving. While we waited for them to finish making pictures of the antique furnishings and luxurious appointments, I had called the front desk in alarm, to be assured that the suite was not included on any tours when it was occupied.

We ate lunch underway as we left Jekyll Island and began winding our way through the rivers and sounds that separated us from Cumberland Island. As we approached Cumberland, we passed uncomfortably close to the Kings Bay Nuclear Submarine

Base. We were shepherded past the entrance by a series of small but heavily armed patrol boats, handed off from one to the next like the baton in a relay race. We could soon see our destination in the distance, but we had a detour of a mile or two around some shallow water to get to the anchorage near the south end of Cumberland Island.

Cumberland Island had once been the exclusive preserve of the Carnegies, who sold it to the government to be used as a national park, with a few constraints. More than 90 percent of the island is now public property, with a few small parcels held by people with life estates; when they die, the balance of the island will become public. The park is referred to as the Cumberland Island National Seashore. The only access is by a ferry, which runs a couple of times per day from nearby St. Mary's, Georgia, or by private vessel. One of the old Carnegie homes is operated as a small, very expensive inn. Otherwise, visitors may camp in managed, semi-improved campsites. There are a few small outbuildings used for displays by the Park Service, but the old mansion is in ruins, as are most of its ancillary structures. There are hiking trails and a few dirt roads crisscrossing the island and there are some 19 miles of unspoiled Atlantic beach.

We dropped our anchor with a few other boats within 100 yards of the Park Service dock, cooked supper, and went to bed early, in anticipation of a full day of hiking the next day.

Cumberland Island

Before the Europeans discovered America, Cumberland Island had been populated for thousands of years by the indigenous people of the area. Early in the era of discovery, Cumberland was a part of Spanish Florida. The Spanish established missions on the several of the big barrier islands along what is now the Georgia coast, including St. Catherine's, St. Simon's, and Cumberland. At first, the impact of the Spanish on the islands was restricted to spreading their brand of Christianity and diseases, to which the local population readily succumbed, being innocent and accepting in the first case, and lacking natural immunities in the second.

As the English colonies began to spread south, encroaching on the Spanish, the Spanish reacted with a military presence. After some years of struggles which extended well beyond these islands, the English prevailed and the Spanish withdrew to the south of the St. Mary's River, which flows into the ocean at the south tip of Cumberland Island. When Oglethorpe founded the English colony of Georgia, he built a hunting lodge, which he named Dungeness, near the south end of Cumberland Island. During the colonial period, plantations occupied the island. From Oglethorpe's day through the American Revolution and up until the Civil War, a series of ever-larger plantation houses occupied the Dungeness site. After sea island cotton was no longer profitable, the plantation house at Dungeness was abandoned until the late 1800s, when Thomas Carnegie, brother of the steel magnate, bought virtually the whole island and built a family retreat, which he called Dungeness, on the site. This last Dungeness was patterned on a Scottish castle and had some 59 rooms, with outbuildings for support functions and some 200 servants. Although Thomas died before it was finished, the Carnegies occupied Dungeness until the Great Depression, when it fell into disuse. This most recent Dungeness burned in 1959, and in the 1970s most of the island was sold to the federal government for use as a national park.

We tied our dinghy to floating dock provided by the Park Service and paid a visitor's fee of a few dollars, giving us free access to the island's public land. Our first stop was Dungeness, of course, where we were amused to see several feral horses grazing among the ruins of what would have presumably been the main hall of the mansion. A bit shy if we got too close, the horses seemed otherwise untroubled by our presence as we poked around. We found ample evidence of former opulence, including the remains of formal gardens. We entertained ourselves at a small museum which housed a few artifacts from various periods of the island's history as well as a collection of photographs from more recent times.

Sufficiently impressed with the wealth of a bygone era, we set out to hike some of the many trails, startling several deer along the way, and pausing to watch a large, pileated woodpecker as it hammered away in the treetops. Much of the island is covered with old growth maritime forest, the lovely oaks, bearded with grey Spanish moss, providing enough shade to minimize the undergrowth. The natural beauty of these parts of the island defies adequate description. The shady, open vistas, softly carpeted with dead and decaying leaves, invited us to wander endlessly through the eerily quiet forest. As it was just two weeks before Christmas, well outside the normal tourist season, we shared the island with only a handful of other visitors, most of whom we never saw. We only knew they were there because we had watched them go ashore at the dock while we were eating our breakfast in the cockpit.

Following the ever-present sound of the surf, we made our way to the beach, stopping often to watch squirrels, raccoons, possums, and armadillos going about their daily activities. We flushed several coveys of quail as we left the shade and crossed the grassy area behind the sand dunes closer to the beach. It was easy to imagine what life would have been like for the original inhabitants; most of what we saw after we left Dungeness appeared to have been untouched by man.

After a few more minutes and one last covey of quail, we crested the sand dunes. The most beautiful beach I've ever seen stretched as far as I could see in either direction. While I'm not a beach-lover, and this was ultimately just a beach like many others along the southeast coast, it was remarkable because there was no trace of development. No boardwalk, no hotdog stands, no lifeguard stands, or bathhouses. We walked north along the beach for about five miles, and we didn't even see a footprint except our own, let alone another person. It's one thing to read that there are 19 miles of pristine beach, but to experience it is otherworldly. To see the miles of undisturbed sand with the surf rolling in while breathing the soft, salty air carried ashore by the gentle sea breeze, the silence unbroken except by the sighing of the wind punctuated by the surf's rhythm was a unique experience for me. Sharing it with my soul-mate and no one else is a memory that I'll keep with me for the rest of my days.

We ate our lunch sitting on a large piece of driftwood, watching the seagulls squabble over the edible tidbits washed up by the surf. Several circled us with interest, eyes fixed on our sandwiches. Knowing better but unable to resist, I tossed a crust into the air as far as I could. As the wind caught it, a gull swooped down and snatched it greedily in midair, flying away at top speed with its treasure as the others chased after it, screaming their indignation. They were so busy fighting over the first crust that they missed the next several crumbs that we tossed on the sand. We soon had a gathering of small shorebirds, eagerly watching for the next treat. They were much less ill-mannered than the gulls, but not quite as entertaining. As we finished our lunch, the gulls returned, circling and screeching as they eyed us expectantly. After a few minutes, they moved on, and we resumed our hike.

Reluctantly, we left the beach, cutting across the dunes to intersect a rough trail that eventually took us back to the west side of the island, where we turned south, back toward Dungeness and the dock. We were surprised anew at all the wildlife we encountered; particularly the number of deer that we spotted grazing peacefully. They appeared almost tame until you took one step in their direction. Even from a distance of 50 to 100 yards that was enough to spook them, and they would disappear as if we had imagined them, taking one or two graceful leaps before blending into the background.

Before we were ready to be there, we found ourselves back at the dock. It was late afternoon, and there were a dozen or so people waiting on the dock with sizable packs, talking among themselves as we walked up. We said hello, and a couple of them chatted with us briefly. They were all in a group of some sort from

St. Mary's, and had spent a long weekend camping on the island, doing what we had been doing. Soon, the ferry came alongside and they shouldered their packs and scrambled aboard to wait for the scheduled departure for the mainland, their adventure over.

We felt fortunate, knowing that our adventure was still just beginning as theirs drew to a close. We climbed into the dinghy and rowed home to rest and think about where we would go next.

Cumberland Island to Melbourne, Fl.

We moved on the next morning, feeling our way through thick fog across Cumberland Sound to the Amelia River. Our GPS gave us precise location information in spite of the fog, which limited our visibility to around 100 feet. I had been navigating by dead reckoning since childhood, long before all the electronics became available, so the ability to plot our actual position on the chart from the GPS instead of relying solely on a compass course and a stop watch to get us to the next channel marker was an unaccustomed luxury for me. We kept our speed down, sounded our fog horn, and listened carefully for any ships or boats close by. We had no company on our trip across the sound, and by the time we entered the Amelia River the fog was beginning to lift. At the fuel dock for the Fernandina Beach, Florida, Municipal Marina, we pulled alongside and tied up, filling our diesel and water tanks as we debated anchoring 100 yards away across the river and coming back to explore the town.

It was a chilly morning, made worse by the lingering damp from the fog. Once we had settled our bill, we decided to move on to the south, hoping to find warmer weather. We pulled away from the dock and followed the Waterway south down the Amelia River, past Amelia Island to the Fort George River. We turned up into the river, edging our way past the shoals until we were able to anchor off the Kingsley Plantation with a few other boats. It was early afternoon, and we considered going ashore to look around the historic site, but there was no floating dock for the dinghy and the tide was falling. Recalling the folks with the stranded dinghy at Fort

Frederica a few days before, we elected to spend the afternoon reading in the cockpit, as the sun that burned the fog away had also brought a little warmth. As it set that evening, with a few wispy cumulus clouds in the sky, we were treated to our first pastel Florida sunset, a fitting end to our first day in the state.

Away early the next morning, we crossed the St. Johns River, busy with shipping traffic bound for the port of Jacksonville, some 15 or 20 miles upstream. Safely across the St. Johns and back in the Waterway, we noticed that our route was becoming inexorably more ditch-like. The Waterway still generally followed natural streams through the noticeably narrower strip of marshland between the barrier islands and the mainland, but the route was arrow-straight for long stretches. We concluded that, unlike the estuaries through South Carolina and Georgia, the streams through here didn't have enough natural depth to make it worthwhile for the Waterway to follow their winding course. If the Corps of Engineers had to dredge for miles on end, they might as well take the shortest, straight-line route.

Except for the large, tacky houses along the way, on this part of the trip we might as well have been driving on an interstate highway. The dredged cuts eventually joined the Tolomato River about ten miles north of St. Augustine, providing us with some relief from the visual monotony for the last few hours before we reached the St. Augustine Inlet. St. Augustine is an interesting place. Founded in 1565, it's the site of the oldest continuously occupied European settlement in North America. Leslie and I had visited by car a few times, and there were some things that we wanted to see and do on this visit.

One of those things was the inevitable chore of laundry, which we had last tackled in Charleston. While the anchorage off the city looked attractive enough, we knew that there was no good place to land our dinghy except at the City Marina. The people who ran the marina knew that, too, and they charged a high enough fee for dinghy access to make it attractive to put the big boat at a slip instead, which also gave us ready access to shoreside showers and the marina's laundry.

We took care of all our chores quickly enough. Leslie did laundry the next morning, while I took advantage of a warm, sunny morning and endless city water to give the boat a thorough wash. The man on the adjacent boat was doing the same thing, and we soon struck up a conversation. His wife was doing laundry as well, and she and Leslie soon appeared on the dock, having met one another in the laundry room while folding clothes.

They were from Canada, recently retired and headed for a winter in the Bahamas. They had owned their boat for many years, having kept it in charter fleets in various places until a few years ago when they had taken it to Canada to get it ready for their retirement cruising. We discovered a number of common interests, and Leslie and I joined them to go grocery shopping, as they had a rental car. We appreciated their offer of a ride, as the store would have been quite a hike, especially for the return trip, laden as we were with groceries.

The next morning, Leslie and I did a bit of sightseeing, visiting a winery and a museum or two. In the afternoon, we saw our new friends in the picnic area at the marina with another couple. The men were chatting, and the newly arrived woman was giving our friend a haircut. Soon, Leslie was perched on the picnic table, getting a trim of her own. I was relieved at that, as she had begun snipping at her hair with the scissors a couple of weeks previously, having felt long overdue for a visit to the hairdresser. Of course, she only cut the parts of her hair that she could see in the mirror and reach with her right hand, so she was beginning to look a bit unbalanced. That was soon remedied at the price of my loaning the woman's husband a tool which he needed for a quick repair on their engine. We enjoyed a dinner with our new friends on their boat and then said goodbye, as we were ready to push farther south the next morning, while they were staying for a while longer in St. Augustine. We promised to watch for one another as we got farther south.

It was getting close to Christmas, when we were planning to meet our daughter in Melbourne, Florida. Leslie's uncle and aunt had recently retired and moved to Melbourne Beach after living in the Boston area since his college days. We were expecting to spend some time with them, too, as we hadn't seen them for a while. We were three days from Melbourne and five days from Christmas, so we didn't dally. We spent one night at anchor in Daytona, and the next night anchored off Titusville. On the night of the 23rd, we anchored in Melbourne, and the next morning, we got ourselves settled in the Melbourne Marina. It turned out to be a friendly, low-key place catering to local boaters more than to transients. We unexpectedly became the center of attention – a new boat from far away, and one in transit, to boot. We were visited and made welcome by many of the marina tenants as they prepared to spend some time on their boats over the holidays.

On Christmas Eve day, we hiked to the Melbourne airport and picked up a rental car. Since our daughter's flight wasn't scheduled to arrive in Orlando until midnight, we drove down to Vero Beach, which would be our next stop on the Waterway once we started traveling again in January. The Vero Beach Municipal Marina is a well-known stop for cruisers; we've heard wonderful things about it for years, so we weren't surprised when we got there to discover that all the cruising folks who were there had gotten together for a potluck Christmas Eve dinner in the middle of the afternoon.

We saw a number of people we had met along the way, including the two couples we had left in St. Augustine a few days earlier. "It got cold," they explained, "so we left." It was markedly warmer in the Melbourne-Vero Beach area. We later learned that it was because that stretch of Florida's coast protrudes well to the east, and the Gulf Stream with its 80-degree water is but a few miles offshore, while it's significantly farther offshore just a few miles to the north near Jacksonville and St. Augustine. Although we had no food to contribute, we were made welcome at the potluck, and we spent an hour or two visiting before we drove back to Melbourne.

After resting on *Play Actor* for a couple of hours, we left for the drive to Orlando. Our daughter's flight arrived on time, and we drove back to the boat and crashed until Christmas morning. Our daughter was enjoying her Christmas break from graduate school, and we had a pleasant family holiday with her and with Leslie's aunt and uncle. The weather was delightful -- cool enough to enjoy wearing a sweater in the evening, and warm enough to enjoy taking it off during the day.

Melbourne to Vero Beach

Restless after a week in Melbourne, we were ready to move on. It had been a treat to spend Christmas with family, and the waters around Melbourne were attractive enough, but we had not seen much of them. When the boat is tied to the dock in a marina, the view never changes, and we were beginning to feel claustrophobic. Sitting on deck, we had no privacy from the people on the docks and nearby boats. At anchor, we were usually 50 to 100 yards from our nearest neighbor, if we had a neighbor at all. In a marina, if we looked out of a porthole, we could only see the next boat, a few short feet away. Although having unlimited water and electricity was nice, we now preferred swinging to our own anchor in an open space.

We also recognized that it was much easier to stick to our budget if we were at anchor. In a marina, we could step off of the boat on a whim and walk to the nearest convenience store, picking up snacks, magazines, and other impulse purchases, not to mention being seductively close to the omnipresent waterfront restaurants with their tantalizing aromas wafting through our open hatches. At anchor, a disciplined approach to spending came much more easily. First, temptation was removed, but of equal importance was the requirement to launch the dinghy and go ashore, which led to planning our excursions and thus our purchases.

Speaking of the dinghy and purchases, we had taken advantage of having a rental car to shop for and buy a small, two-horsepower outboard engine, so we no longer had to row the dinghy. Rowing is good exercise, and it's something that we enjoy, but we had come to realize that there would be places where we had to cover a considerable distance from our anchorage to land the dinghy. Usually, that meant that we would be exposed to wind, current, and choppy water, as well. Norfolk had been like that, and we had recognized that if we had been at anchor in Charleston, it would have been the same. Rowing the dinghy any distance under those conditions made for a slow, tiring trip. Now we had an outboard, significantly increasing our mobility when we were at anchor. Although we had tested it briefly in Melbourne, riding around the marina in the dinghy, our first chance to really use the new engine would be in Vero Beach.

When we had settled our bill with the marina and were ready to leave, we realized that a persistent northerly wind had reduced the water level in the marina basin by 18 inches, leaving us aground in our slip. With our long, full keel, we were stuck firmly enough that the engine wouldn't move us. Learning from the dock master that there was deeper water just a few feet behind us, we ran long lines to some pilings across the fairway and attached them to our two primary winches, normally used for trimming the larger sails. We used the winches to pull *Play Actor* out to deeper water. With a delay of only half an hour, we were on our way to Vero Beach.

The character of the Waterway had changed yet again on our way from St. Augustine to Daytona. The familiar marshlands were behind us. The channel was still dredged in long, straight stretches through very shallow water trapped between the barrier islands and the mainland, but the bottom was no longer as muddy. It was mostly sand, with hard, exposed patches of limestone in the places where the sand had been washed away. The shoreline, while still low, was lined with mangrove swamps rather than with marshlands, and the breadth of the shallows from shore to shore was often as much as a couple of miles. It was even wider as we passed to the west of the Cape Canaveral complex, where from a distance of several miles, we could see the space shuttle poised on a launching pad, dwarfing everything on the flat horizon. Except in the narrow parts, particularly south of Canaveral, we found this area to be less attractive than the earlier parts of the Waterway. In the narrow parts, waterfront development broke the monotony, but was in itself not very attractive. Had we been closer to the mangroves as we crossed the broader, undeveloped reaches, no doubt we would have seen some interesting wildlife. Since most of the water is between one and three feet in depth, our draft confined us to the dredged channel, where there wasn't much to see.

As we drew near to Vero Beach, the broad, lagoon-like Indian River began to be filled with small mangrove islands and the channel curved around them. We were passing through an interesting, almost jungle-like area, broken by occasional development as the channel passed close to either the mainland or the barrier island in its serpentine course. As we came to the Vero Beach Bridge, we turned back sharply to the northeast. We rounded a point of mangroves and entered the mooring basin of the Vero Beach Municipal Marina.

Vero Beach has made an effort to offer warm hospitality to cruising boats for a long time, and as a result, the marina is always crowded. In earlier times, the broad, deep pool in the mangroves made a fine anchorage, convenient to the marina's facilities. In recent years, the city placed moorings in the old anchorage as a way to accommodate more visitors than the marina could squeeze into its limited dock space. A mooring is nothing more than an extremely heavy, semi-permanent anchor with a length of heavy chain sufficient to reach the surface of the water with just a little slack. The chain is terminated by a large float, commonly called a mooring buoy or a mooring ball, to which the bow of a boat is tied with a relatively short length of rope, called a mooring pennant.

Because of the massive weight of the mooring system, a boat attached to a mooring will swing in a circle with a radius of just a little more than the boat's length, as opposed to a circle with a radius of about seven times the depth of the water for a properly anchored boat riding to its own anchor. Thus the city's mooring field made it possible to pack many more visiting boats safely into the limited space of the anchorage. For the use of a mooring, the city charged a nominal fee of a few dollars per night. Payment of the fee entitled the crew of a visiting boat to use all the marina's facilities, including telephone jacks in the lounge, enabling visitors with laptop computers to check email.

The marina was such a popular stop during the peak winter season that there weren't enough moorings for all the visiting boats. The harbormaster solved this problem by assigning up to three boats to each mooring. The first boat in would tie up to the mooring pennant, and the other two would put out fenders along one side and tie alongside the first boat, which would end up as the center boat of a three-boat raft. Although this offered less privacy than being anchored, it was as private as being tied to a dock, at a small fraction of the cost. It offered almost all the amenities of dockage except electricity, which most cruising boats didn't really need. Of course, fresh water had to be brought in jugs from shore using a dinghy, but this was a minor inconvenience, and it was offset by better ventilation than found at a dock, as the rafted boats were free to swing into the breeze.

We stayed at Vero Beach for ten days and thoroughly enjoyed ourselves. Our friends from St. Augustine were still there, and we met a number of other people as we availed ourselves of the marina's facilities. The City of Vero Beach, which catered heavily to retirees, offered a free shuttle bus system which we used to get around town. It made the city an attractive spot for an extended visit, and we learned that some boaters literally spent the entire winter at moorings in the marina. The beach was a ten-minute walk; for those who chose not to walk, there was a shuttle bus to the beach a couple of times every hour. There was a nice shopping mall, hardware stores, marine supply stores, grocery stores and innumerable restaurants for every taste and price, all within walking distance or a short, free bus ride. Some people referred to the town as Velcro Beach because it was so easy to get stuck there.

We stayed as long as we did partly to visit a bit more with Leslie's aunt and uncle. Their home was about a 20-minute drive, and of course, they had a car. We also took advantage of the easy access to shopping to handle a number of minor repairs and improvements to Play Actor, stocking up on groceries all the while. We would have a couple of more opportunities to buy groceries before we left Miami for the Bahamas, but none that offered the convenience of Vero Beach.

We made our first-ever visit to that quintessential American shopping Mecca, Walmart, while we were in Vero Beach. As unlikely as it seems, we had never lived within easy reach of a Walmart; we had always lived in urban surroundings, far from the suburban areas favored by Walmart. Our neighbors in the marina were constantly making Walmart runs to stock up on all sorts of things, some of which puzzled us.

We had seen more than one couple returning to boats with multiple case lots of paper towels and toilet paper, for example. When we asked why, the veterans of time in the Bahamas patiently explained that paper towels and toilet paper were *very* expensive in the Bahamas. We wondered but didn't ask what their rate of consumption was on those items, thinking of our own. In three months, we might use three rolls of paper towels, and two or three times as many rolls of toilet paper. Either those folks had substantially different habits, or they were planning on staying for several years. We never discovered which it was.

Although we didn't have a particular requirement that took us there, we decided to go to Walmart just to see what the fuss was about. We were stunned at what we saw. The carnival-like atmosphere of the immense store seemed to spill out onto the sidewalk, with tables and displays of after-Christmas sale merchandise. When we entered the store, we were struck by the sheer size of the place; it was overwhelming. The idea that there were several fast food franchises inside offering all sorts of unhealthy things to eat amazed us, and we watched as people from widely dispersed economic strata pushed and shoved to fill their carts with all sorts of stuff.

After we got over the initial shock, we wandered the aisles, examining the merchandise, noticing that things that purported to be wonderful deals on name-brand merchandise weren't quite what they appeared to be. Either the price was inflated and discounted, or the goods were just slightly different from those of the same brand available elsewhere at a slightly higher price. Clearly, a lot of items were attractively priced, but there was nothing we needed. We left without buying anything, waiting for the bus back to the marina with a number of other people who were obviously boaters bound for the Bahamas. We could tell by the case lots of paper towels and toilet paper.

Vero Beach to Miami

The night before we left Vero Beach, we studied the charts and realized that in the 140 miles to Miami, there were some 45 drawbridges, most of which opened only at certain times. The Waterway itself had already become unattractive to us, so we elected to leave the Ditch in favor of sailing offshore for the rest of our trip down the East Coast. The weather was warm and settled, and in the ocean we had the hope of actually sailing instead of running the diesel. The nearest inlet that was passable was at Fort Pierce, about 15 miles to the south. Beyond Fort Pierce, it was 45 miles to the Lake Worth Inlet, and Port Everglades Inlet at Fort Lauderdale was 50 miles beyond that. From the Port Everglades Inlet, the distance to Miami's Government Cut Inlet was a bit over 20 miles. The 45 miles from Fort Pierce Inlet to Lake Worth Inlet would be an easy day, and both inlets were deep and well marked, used by ocean going ships, as were Port Everglades and Miami.

We left Vero Beach by ourselves in the late morning to make the 15-mile trip to Fort Pierce, where we planned to anchor just inside the inlet for an early departure the next morning. None of our friends from Vero Beach were going to venture into the ocean; they planned to take the Waterway as far south as possible, staying in protected waters. By mid-afternoon we were comfortably anchored among some man-made islands where the dredges had dumped the sand and muck from clearing the ship channel to the Fort Pierce Inlet. We were about a 30-minute run from the ocean, and we lazed away the afternoon watching local sport fishermen catching redfish around the islands.

The next morning dawned with dense fog; it was several hours before we could see well enough to work our way out of the anchorage. There were no channel markers to get us back to the junction of the Waterway and the inlet channel. By the time the fog lifted, we thought it was too late to leave and get into Lake Worth before dark. While we knew from the charts that the inlet channel was well-lighted, we would have to try to find a spot to anchor in the dark. That wasn't appealing, as we expected that the anchorage would be crowded. We spent another night where we were and left at the break of day the next morning.

As we motored from the Waterway into the inlet in the gray light of dawn, the fog closed in again. By then, though, we were in the deep, straight, well-marked inlet channel. We elected to follow it out to sea, knowing that once in open water, offshore, the only hazards would be from ships and other small boats, which we would be able to see or at least hear well enough to avoid them. By the time the fog lifted at about nine o'clock, we were well on our way. We had neither heard nor seen any other traffic, and we had a nice offshore breeze. We shut down the engine and raised the sails, making it into the Lake Worth anchorage comfortably before sunset. The sighing of the pure, sweet sea breeze as it filled our sails and sent us slicing quietly through the clear, blue-green water was pure joy after several months in the Ditch, listening to the diesel for hours every time we were underway.

We left at dawn again the next day, to find a clear morning and a nice breeze to carry us along a few miles offshore. We were pleased with the clear, blue-green water around us after months of the always dark, sometimes muddy water that we had found in the Waterway. We weren't sure as we sailed along whether we would stop in Fort Lauderdale that night, or whether we would sail on to Miami. As we finished our lunch, we were just north of the Port Everglades Inlet. It was an easy choice to keep sailing; we would make Miami at about sunset. While we would have to find a spot to anchor in the dark, that didn't appear to be much of a challenge from looking at the charts. There was a great deal of well-protected water among the man-made Venetian Islands just to the north of the causeway that formed the north bank of the ship channel from Government Cut to the port of Miami.

As we made our decision, we heard several of our friends from Vero Beach talking on the radio. We called them and learned that they were still a few hours north of Fort Lauderdale, on their painstaking way south down the Waterway, waiting for all those drawbridges. They planned to spend the night somewhere between Lake Worth and Fort Lauderdale, and would spend the next night in Fort Lauderdale. They expected to arrive in Miami the day after tomorrow. They were envious when they heard that we were having a beautiful sail, and still more envious to hear that we would spend tonight in Miami.

The wind dropped, and we hit a little unfavorable current in the last few miles, so it was fully dark when we entered the marked ship channel into Miami's Government Cut. As we left the ship channel and turned north along the Waterway to look for a spot to anchor, we were awestruck to see that the 65-foot-high bridge that spanned the Waterway just north of the ship channel was lit from underneath with pastel blue spot lights. We turned and looked behind us to see that the companion span a hundred yards or so to the south was lit with pastel pink lights. Miami was clearly a city concerned with aesthetics. We then began to notice slowly changing pastel lighting that put all the city's tall buildings into stark relief against the black, star-studded sky. It was so pretty that we were distracted from our quest to find the area where the charts showed adequate water for us to turn in among the Venetian Islands for our planned anchorage. Even so, we found a satisfactory spot and were settled soon enough to have dinner and go to bed by 10:00 p.m.

The sounds of the city coming to life woke us up a little after sunrise the next morning, and we sat in the cockpit with our coffee, looking around and trying to get our bearings. I spotted a time and temperature sign atop a nearby bank building and watched as it changed from "6:40 a.m." to "72 degrees." It was mid-January, and we were sitting outside in the early morning, drinking coffee in our summer-weight pajamas. We basked in our contentment for a while and then had breakfast. Once we were dressed, we pulled up the anchor and moved a bit farther from the Waterway and downtown Miami. We picked out an area with plenty of room to anchor that put us within a 100-yard dinghy trip of the Miami Yacht Club, which we knew welcomed visiting cruisers. Their dinghy dock would provide a secure place for us to leave the dinghy while we explored.

By the time our friends arrived two days later, we were well acquainted with the club and with South Beach, a 20-minute dinghy ride away. The club had a nice bar and restaurant, as well as a swimming pool and a telephone line that we could use for email access. Based on our membership in a yacht club in Maryland, the Miami Yacht Club granted us reciprocal privileges for a small daily fee, and we soon felt quite at home there.

South Beach, besides the obvious beach, put everything we could think of within easy reach. Grocery stores and restaurants, coffee shops, bookstores, and some of the most stunningly attractive people we've ever seen kept us endlessly amused. We spent two weeks enjoying ourselves, half-heartedly watching for a few days of favorable weather during which we could cross the Gulf Stream to Bimini, which would be our first landfall in the Bahamas. There was an excellent marine supply store at the south end of South Beach where we picked up a few last-minute items, but we spent most of our time watching the beautiful people and admiring the Art Deco buildings.

One place that quickly became a favorite spot to while away a few hours was the Lincoln Road Mall. Formerly the main east-west street in Miami Beach, it had been closed to traffic and turned into a park of sorts. It was perhaps 75 yards wide, and expensive shops and restaurants lined both sides. Many had outdoor tables on the Mall with handsome waiters and beautiful waitresses shuttling back and forth with trays of delicacies for their patrons. On the weekends, stalls were set up on the Mall, and vendors sold everything from fresh fruits and vegetables to arts, crafts, clothing, and expensive jewelry.

In the midst of all this, young people with well-toned, tanned, and artfully displayed bodies wandered, clearly taking a break from time on the beach. They came in an array of colors and sizes and sometimes were of indeterminate gender, but their mere appearance would have caused an upheaval anywhere else. Here, only the tourists from the mid-west in their Mickey Mouse T-shirts noticed them. One quintessential South Beach scene has stayed with us for all the years since that first visit.

There was handsome young man tending a stall on the Mall, where he sold handmade wooden roses. Each petal was exquisitely carved and painted before being fastened to an equally realistic stem. No two were alike, and it took careful scrutiny to determine that they weren't real. He had a few that were perfumed that he kept near to hand, and if people paused to look, he would hold one out for them to sniff. One older couple had been drawn in by his polite smile and nod, and as the woman sniffed the flower he held under her nose, she closed her eyes for a moment. She reached for his brown hand with her lily white one, grasping it and pulling the flower close again to examine it. "At first, I thought these were artificial. They're almost too perfect to be real," she said.

He smiled engagingly and put the flower back in its bud vase on the counter. She moved closer, examining the displays of artfully arranged, colorful roses as the vendor and her male companion watched. After a moment, she looked up at the vendor. "They *are* real, aren't they?" She looked hopeful as she waited a few beats for his answer.

As he was about to answer, an impossibly buxom, well-tanned, young blond woman in a nearly non-existent string bikini bounded past, slipping smoothly between the old lady and her husband, who stared transfixed at the glorious apparition bouncing along on some sort of spring-loaded, pogo stick-like boots that lifted her a couple of feet into the air with every six or seven-foot stride. The woman had missed the girl passing behind her, but the vendor and the woman's husband both paused, their eyes hungrily caressing each of the girl's rippling, well-defined muscles as they gleamed with coconut-scented suntan oil. While the woman's husband stared after the dazzling girl, his mouth gaping and eyes bulging, the vendor glanced at the old man, shook his head, and smiled. "Ma'am, sir," he said, "remember, this is South Beach. Nothing you see is real." The woman took the carved flower and handed the young man a $20 bill as her husband nodded absently, sniffing at the lingering scent of coconut oil.

Miami to Bimini, the Bahamas

Bimini is about 45 miles across the Gulf Stream from Miami, but distance doesn't tell the whole story. The Gulf Stream moves around; its precise boundaries are ever-changing, depending on weather patterns and tides. Usually, its western wall is only a couple of miles east of the sea buoy marking the Miami entrance, and its current flows from south to north with a velocity that sometimes approaches four knots over the ground. The Gulf Stream has been likened to a mighty river that flows through the sea. The eastern wall of the stream touches Bimini; to get there, we had to cross that river, which flows north at four knots, in a boat that wouldn't go much faster than the current. The normal cruising speed of a boat like ours is around six knots, but that's the speed through the water. If we steer directly into a four-knot current, our speed over the ground is reduced to two knots. Conversely, if we turn around and sail with the current at our backs, our speed over the ground rises to ten knots.

Ignoring the Gulf Stream, our compass course from Miami to Bimini would have been approximately due east, but if we had steered due east, the current of the Gulf Stream would have pushed us to the north at four knots while we were going east at six knots. After 45 miles of that, we would have ended up many miles to the north of our desired destination. This is a relatively simple navigation problem and we knew well how to solve it. The solution was to steer a course that was very close to southeast, and that pointed our bow at an angle into the current for the entire trip. We knew that the Gulf Stream would slow us down significantly.

We calculated that our effective speed over the ground from Miami to Bimini would be less than four knots, so we estimated that under ideal conditions, the crossing would take about 12 hours. Experienced sailors know better than to plan on ideal conditions; we were crossing open water at a time of year when the weather could change dramatically in a few hours. We also needed to arrive in daylight, as aids to navigation in the Bahamas are a sometime thing. To get through the shoaling, changeable Bimini entrance channel, we would need good daylight, so we went to bed at dark the night before our departure, and we left the anchorage in Miami at 1:00 a.m. Our Gulf Stream crossing was unremarkable. We were tied up in a marina in Bimini in time to clear in with Customs and Immigration before they closed for the day.

Bimini is separated from Florida by more than distance; it's a whole world away. While many have heard of it, it's not much of a tourist destination. The popular tourist spots in the Bahamas could easily be mistaken for parts of the U.S. That's not true of Bimini; the only activities that attract tourists to Bimini are big game fishing and scuba diving, although even scuba diving didn't attract very many folks at the time we were there.

Bimini, at the time we visited, was almost deserted during the week. On the weekends, people in big, fast boats came from south Florida to fish and party. A few tourists flew in on Chalk Airlines; the little seaplanes landed in the harbor a few hundred feet from our boat. We had watched the planes take off from the Government Cut ship channel near where we had been anchored in Miami.

The visitors spent their time fishing or scuba diving from the fleet of charter boats in the harbor, and they spent the evenings at the Compleat Angler, listening to a local calypso band and admiring the Hemingway memorabilia after dining at one of the tourist restaurants like the Anchorage. Ernest Hemingway lived at the Anchorage while he wrote *To Have and Have Not*. Sometime after that, the cottage became a restaurant, trading on Hemingway's former presence.

Hemingway had been fond of Bimini, and Bimini still remembered him. The whole of Alice Town, Bimini, was like a shrine to Hemingway, and it would not have been a surprise to encounter him in any of the little open-air, dirt-floored bars along King's Highway, Alice Town's one street. The bars doubtless looked much as they had when he was in residence.

Bimini was always a haven for smugglers. It's actually a cluster of small islands, closer to the mainland of the U.S. than it is to the rest of the Bahamas. From a law-enforcement perspective, it's a sort of no-man's land, and it thrived during the Prohibition era, enjoying another economic surge in the 80s from the drug trade.

By the time we visited, the drug runners had moved on to more efficient means of shipment, although there was ample evidence that small-time smuggling was still an active pursuit. Duty-free rum for a few dollars a liter and Cuban cigars, illegal in the U.S., were readily available to tempt the boaters from Florida. More nefarious items were rumored to be at hand, as well. In passing time with some of the locals, we learned that things were relatively quiet in Bimini these days, although just a few years earlier, gunfights between drug dealers along King's Highway had been a common occurrence.

We explored the island on foot, walking from the south end all the way to the north end. As we passed through Bailey Town, which was much more residential than Alice Town, we made note of a hand-lettered cardboard sign hanging outside a loosely fenced compound. The sign offered stuffed lobster dinners for $10 on Sunday night. I checked my watch and discovered that it was Sunday.

We studied the establishment for a few minutes, noticing that it looked deserted. It comprised about an acre, with a few strands of broken barbed wire draped casually around the perimeter. Just to the left of the driveway entrance, there was a shack about 12 feet square. It sat on concrete blocks and had a large padlock on the door. Goats and chickens foraged among the weeds and dust. There were a few partly dismantled, wrecked automobiles in the yard, along with some small boats and large, rusty appliances.

At the back of the lot was a two-storey structure that vaguely resembled a suburban split-level house assembled from mismatched materials. High on the front of the house was a large sign proclaiming it to be "Tiger and Pat's – hardware, building materials, groceries, auto & appliance parts and repairs, and plumbing supplies." We decided to return later and try the lobster.

We walked back to "Tiger and Pat's" an hour or so after sundown, accompanied by two friends from another boat. There were dim lights scattered around the yard and the door to the small shack was open. The inside of the shack was brightly lighted. We went up a few rickety steps and found ourselves in a tiny grocery store, well stocked with canned goods and liquor. There was a pleasant-looking woman behind a small counter.

"Good evening," she said.

"Good evening. How are you?" I asked.

"Fine. And you folks?"

"We're well, thanks."

"Can I help you find something?" she offered.

"Are we too late for the lobster dinner?"

"No. You want four dinners?"

"Yes, please."

"I will get them. Cold drinks are in the refrigerator. You may help yourselves," she said, gesturing to a rusty old household refrigerator in one corner, her carefully enunciated British English incongruous with the setting.

She went through an unnoticed door into a tiny, adjoining kitchen and began assembling our dinners, loading an incredible amount of food into Styrofoam containers. She brought them back in a few minutes and collected our money, suggesting that we have a seat outside as she flipped some light switches.

We went outside to discover a large cable spool tipped on its side under a tree, now brightly lighted by bulbs dangling from the limbs. The makeshift table was surrounded by barstools. We settled on the stools and opened our containers to find that we each had a huge stuffed lobster tail, mounds of peas and rice, and fresh green salad. As we tucked in, a musical rumble came from the shadows nearby.

I glanced up to see a giant emerging from the dark, singing "Swing Low, Sweet Chariot" as he shuffled his feet in what I would have called a Gullah 'shout' in my youth. Back in the days of slavery, rigid Baptists had forbidden dancing, but their strictures were circumvented by the expedient of 'shouting' prayers with rhythmic motions of feet, hands, and bodies. This man's movements were familiar to a boy from Geechee country. He concluded his performance to our soft applause, bowed modestly, and introduced himself.

"Welcome, and good evening," the big man said, in a smooth, almost impossibly deep, melodious voice. "I'm Tiger. My wife, Pat, made your dinner. We're glad you are here in Bimini with us. Are you enjoying your visit?"

"Certainly, we are," Leslie responded.

"Good," he boomed, nodding. "Bimini is mostly peaceful, now, but if anybody bothers you, you just tell them that Tiger looks after you. Then no one will bother you, I promise."

"Thank you, Tiger," I said.

"You are welcome. Enjoy your dinner, and if you are here next Sunday, come and hear me preach at the Baptist church overlooking the beach. We would be pleased to have you visit."

And with that, he faded back into the darkness, leaving us to reflect upon the diverse skills bred by life on a small island, and the fellowship that extended to all who ventured off the tourist path.

****

We quickly adjusted to the pace of life in Bimini. One Sunday morning, I was relaxing by the pool at the Bimini Bluewater Marina when two bleached-blond women intruded upon my solitude. Leslie was aboard the boat, absorbed in her book, unaware of the two heavily made-up, scantily clad sharks circling her husband. The scent of perfume was almost overcome by the more pleasant, less incongruous aroma of suntan oil.

"Where are you from?" one of them asked me.

"Well, ..." I said, in a down-island tempo, looking surreptitiously for an escape route.

"C'mon! That's not a hard question. Where do you live?" she asked impatiently, her speech dripping New York.

I was rescued by an older Bahamian man who was sitting nearby, enjoying a rum and Coke. "De mon, he live on de green boat, jus' da," he explained, gesturing toward the dock to show which green boat he meant.

"Yeah, but where do you *live*, really?"

"Where de green boat set. Jus' now in Bimini, I t'ink," I answered, slipping into the local patois.

The old man nodded, sipping his rum drink and grinning a gap-toothed grin. "He here wit' he lovely young wife," he added, giving me a subtle wink. The woman picked up her book and pointedly began a whispered conversation with her companion. Occasionally, one of them would glare at me or the old man. After a few minutes, they gathered up their things and left.

"De ladies, dey from New York. Push-push. Dey come to relax, but dey don' know relax," the old man said.

Bimini to Chubb Cay

Bimini was a useful stop. In our two weeks there, we got into the rhythm of island life much more smoothly than we would have in the more common stops like Nassau or Freeport. We finally decided to move during a period when the persistent northerly winds had dropped to a whisper, having learned that this time of year we shouldn't squander an opportunity for a smooth crossing of the Great Bahama Bank to Chubb Cay.

The Great Bahama Bank is an undersea plateau some 70 miles wide that stretches east from Bimini to the Berry islands. Most of the Bank is covered in gin-clear water ranging in depth from eight to 12 feet, with occasional small areas of deeper or shallower water. In relatively calm conditions, such as the ones we chose for our crossing, it was eerily like sailing in a swimming pool. As we ghosted along, propelled by a light breeze, we whiled away the hours peering over the side, watching the clean, sandy bottom slide smoothly beneath our keel. We saw fish, conch, and starfish. There were random patches of sea grass, but for most of our trip the bottom was clean sand with a few patch reefs.

In unsettled weather, traversing the Bank could be a less pleasant experience, as we were about to learn. Because there is some dangerously shallow water immediately to the east of the Bimini Islands, we had been forced to wait until the sun was high to leave Bimini and sail onto the Bank. There are no channel markers; you navigate by eye, watching for reefs in the clear water as you work your way onto the Bank, judging the depth ahead by the color of the water.

Our late departure meant that we couldn't make it all the way across the Bank in daylight, so a little before sunset, we sailed a mile or so south of the straight line course from Bimini to Chub Cay. Anchoring directly on the course line is dangerous, as large motor yachts sometimes cross the Bank at night. They draw less water than *Play Actor*, and as there are no generally no obstructions, they travel at high speed, often steered by an autopilot, while the crew maintains only a casual lookout. Although we were well-lit, we deemed it prudent to get off the beaten path to stop for the night.

As eerily beautiful as the day's sail had been, it didn't compare to anchoring in nine feet of clear water, far out of sight of land. We ate a simple dinner in the cockpit while watching the sun set across the open sea. Sunsets at sea are never mundane; if the sky is cloudy, the clouds are illuminated from below by reflected light from over the horizon, glowing in shades from pastel pinks to bloody crimson. If the sky is clear, the low angle reflected rays are dazzling until the sun drops below the horizon and winks out in a flash of green light.

Pleasantly tired from our sail, we were soon asleep, but not for long. We woke up after a few hours to the howl of a north wind in our rigging. As the wind drove the shallow water before it, steep, short waves quickly formed. *Play Actor* bucked and reared erratically and we got little sleep for the rest of the night. We were away as soon as there was enough light for us to see what we were doing on deck. The wind had clocked from north to northeast, so we were now smashing into the wind-driven waves, spray flying and the boat heeled well over to starboard, close hauled in something over 20 knots of apparent wind. While the ride wasn't as pleasant as it had been the day before, we were making better time, and it was just shortly after lunch that we anchored in the protection of Chubb Cay.

Our Canadian friends from St. Augustine had left Bimini with us, but having a lighter boat, they didn't keep pace with us in the rough conditions, so they arrived about an hour and a half behind us. We launched our dinghies and the four of us went ashore to look around. There was a marina at Chubb Cay catering to big sport fishing boats, although it was sparsely occupied. While we were tying up the dinghies, a local fisherman in an open boat offered to sell us fresh conch, gesturing to show us his catch, which was spread out in the bottom of his boat. We agreed to buy some, feebly attempting to negotiate. "How much for enough to feed the four of us?" I asked, without a clue as to the going rate for conch.

He shrugged by way of answering me. "Fresh. I clean for you."

"Ten dollars?" I said, remembering the price of the conch fritters we had enjoyed at the Anchorage Restaurant in Bimini.

"You pay me now?"

I took a $10 bill from my wallet and extended it toward him, holding tightly to my end as he took the other between thickly calloused fingers. "How long to clean them?" I asked.

"You go to the restaurant?" he asked.

I shook my head. "We're just going to look around."

He nodded. "Ready when you back."

I released the $10, and we walked away as he gestured to a young boy lounging in the shade nearby. I watched from the corner of my eye as the boy took the $10, listened for a moment, nodded, and scampered away. "That $10 is gone," our Canadian friend said. "You won't see it again."

We wandered around the marina grounds, stopping in the office to visit with the manager, who offered us the use of a phone line if we wanted to collect our email later. That was a relief, because we had discovered in Bimini that our cell phones didn't work, and we had been unable to find anywhere with a phone line into which we could plug a modem. We had been completely cut off from the states, except for a few brief, expensive credit card calls on marginally functioning Bahamian pay phones to let people know we were alive.

This inability to communicate was something that had taken us by surprise. We had a cell phone modem (Remember dial-up modems?) in our laptop, which we had used often along the Waterway when we couldn't find a place offering a phone jack for email. We had been assured by our carrier that we had international roaming and that our cell phone would work in the Bahamas. The Bahamian government's telephone company, Batelco, didn't agree. "Too much cell phone fraud," they had told us when we inquired at their office in Bimini. "We jus' don' do roaming." Our questions about buying a Batelco cell phone had drawn a response of, "No, too expensive." When we asked the price, the answer was a shrug.

We continued to explore outside the marina gates, finding a local bar and nightclub that appeared to be out of business. Besides the club, we found a few sleepy-looking local businesses, mostly offering boat maintenance or repairs. We walked back up to the dinghy dock, where we found three men sitting in the boat with the fisherman who had taken my $10, passing a half-empty bottle of rum from hand to hand.

"Hey, Captain! Conch ready," the fisherman greeted us, hefting a bulging plastic grocery bag as he rose unsteadily to his feet. "Friends help clean," he explained, passing me the bag as he gestured at the other men in his boat. They all nodded at us, grinning happily as they passed the bottle around again.

I nodded back, noticing as I took the bag that there were no more conch in the boat, and spotting a pile of shells on the bottom, visible through the clear water alongside the dock. "Thank you, gentlemen," I said still surprised at the heft of the bag.

"Welcome to Chubb Cay, Captain. We hope you enjoy de visit, an' de conch." His companions nodded again and passed the bottle.

The four of us went back to our boats and divided up the meat, estimating that we probably had in excess of ten pounds of fresh conch. We had conch fritters for dinner and studied every recipe we could find. Over the next few days, we had fried cracked conch (cracked, as in beaten with a hammer; it's tough meat), marinated grilled conch, conch chowder, conch ceviche, and several other preparations that we devised ourselves in an effort to finish the seemingly endless supply of conch meat. Our Canadian friend was right about one thing, though. We never saw that $10 bill again.

Chubb Cay to George Town, Exumas

We spent two months exploring the central and southern Bahamas. From Chubb Cay, we spent several days working our way south as far as George Town, in the Exumas, where we stayed for almost a month, trapped by unexpectedly severe winter weather. We grew tired of George Town after a few days, but we were stuck there. Its harbor was large, and one of the few that offered reasonable protection from the frequent winter storms that blew through with winds of close to 30 knots from the northwest through the northeast. Many of the other Bahamian anchorages that we had visited would have been uncomfortable or even dangerous in those conditions.

Even in George Town, there were periods of several days when we didn't leave the boat. Aside from the prospect of a wet, unpleasant dinghy ride to town, the anchorage was uncomfortably crowded, and boats frequently blew through the anchorage when their anchors broke loose from the winds and rough water. When that happened, the anchor of the dragging boat would often foul the anchors of one or more nearby boats, creating a chain reaction of havoc. When the wind was up, we wanted to be aboard *Play Actor* to protect her from our neighbors' boats.

The nasty weather notwithstanding, we enjoyed our time in the Bahamas, although it was not what we had expected. The country includes about 700 islands and cays; most are small and uninhabited. Most of them have no natural source of fresh water, and nearly all are low and sandy, with inhospitable outcroppings of sharp limestone. Agriculture is non-existent on most of the islands;

except for seafood, goats, and chicken, food was imported and very expensive, not to mention being somewhat scarce. We learned to like the local diet of dried beans, rice, seafood, and canned vegetables, supplemented occasionally with some stringy, local chicken or goat meat. In the larger places, there was usually a reasonable selection of frozen meat and some fresh vegetables and fruit, but at exorbitant prices.

Nassau, located on New Providence Island, is the nation's capital and has a population of about 250,000 people; the population of the whole country is less than 350,000. The next largest center of population after Nassau is on Grand Bahama Island, with about 50,000 people living in Freeport and West End. In the Abacos, in the northern Bahamas, there are a few towns with between 1,000 and 5,000 residents. Visualize the remaining few people spread over the 25 to 30 islands that are inhabited. Alice Town, Bimini, and George Town, Exumas, with about a thousand people each, are major centers of population.

When we were in George Town, the official estimate of the population was 800 people, many of whom lived outside the town. During the period of our stay, there were 450 cruising sailboats officially registered with the harbormaster, each with two or more people aboard. The visitors outnumbered the local population, and with their relative wealth and demand for premium goods and boat repair services, they had a substantial impact on the local economy. The impact was not always positive; if the mail boat didn't show up as scheduled, there were shortages of food, fuel, and other goods.

Fresh water was scarce, as well, and the profligate use of water by the visitors severely taxed the local supply. There was a public tap at one of the dinghy docks where it was possible to fill jugs with water that was brackish and brown-tinged, but considered potable. It wasn't unusual to find a mere trickle coming out of the tap. We had begun catching rainwater early in our cruising, so we weren't particularly troubled by this, but our fellow visitors would line up in the mornings with their jugs, hoping for more than a trickle. People who had reverse osmosis desalination systems aboard their boats didn't want to run them, as the water in the overcrowded harbor was often foul, and diesel fuel to power their water-makers was very expensive, not to mention sometimes scarce.

The weather finally broke, and we started making our way back to the north, stopping only as we needed to rest. We fell in with friends on another boat for part of the trip, and anchored early one afternoon at Norman's Cay, an easy day's sail from Nassau, where we planned to stop for fuel before departing for the states. Norman's Cay had been occupied and turned into an armed camp by a drug lord in the 80s. He had taken over a resort by force of arms, paying the property owners an absurdly high price, but allowing them no option but to sell and leave.

What attracted him was apparently the island's airport, with a relatively long runway, which had become his base for consolidating shipments to the U.S. market. The wreckage of a DC-3 was partially submerged in the lagoon in the center of the island, an indication of the scale of his operation. The condo development where he had made his headquarters was in ruins, but his office was still there, strewn with papers, mostly shipping documents, presumably false. From his lookout tower above the office, we had a 360-degree view of the island, and we could see a similar tower on the next island to the north, where the DEA had maintained an outpost to monitor his shipments.

He had paid off the Bahamian government for several years to maintain his transshipment point on Norman's Cay, carrying on his business in plain sight of the frustrated DEA agents, who had no authority to interfere. Finally, the crooked politicians had been voted out of office, and the drug lord left in the middle of the night, eventually to be extradited from Columbia and imprisoned in the U.S. The original owners had never reclaimed their property, not that we blamed them. The experience of walking around Norman's Cay was a sobering illustration of the magnitude of the illicit trade in drugs, and we found it a little frightening to realize that something so wrong had taken place so recently, and so close to home.

The next day, we had sailed on to Nassau; we wanted to stop in a marina, as we both craved long, hot showers. We had not enjoyed that luxury for a couple of months. As we approached Nassau, we began calling marinas on the VHF radio, only to discover that they were all full, with the exception of the new, luxury marina at the Atlantis Resort, which had space for us, but would charge us $150 per night, approximately five times what the other places charged. We debated it briefly and decided to do it; we had spent very little money for the last two months, as there was nothing on which to spend it.

By late afternoon, we pulled into our designated slip at Atlantis; our little boat looked out of place in the 100-foot-long, 50-foot-wide slip. Clearly, Atlantis didn't cater to our end of the yachting market. Several attractive young men and women in khaki shorts and brilliant white polo shirts took our dock lines and connected our shore power cord, just as if we belonged there. As they finished and climbed into a golf cart on the dock, another attractive young woman pulled up in another golf cart. She got out with a clipboard in hand and signed us in, offering brochures for the casino and the restaurants, and explaining that the full room service menu from the hotel was available for delivery to *Play Actor,* 24 hours a day. She handed over two key cards, embossed with our boat name; she told us that they would provide access to 'guest only' facilities, as well as allowing us to charge any purchases to our account. "Do you have any questions?" she asked.

"Where are the showers?" Leslie wanted to know.

"In the marina's spa; when you're ready, just call the office and I'll come pick you up and drive you there."

Leslie glanced at me. "I'm ready," she said. "You ready?"

"Let me grab our towels," I said, starting below.

"Towels are provided; you only need any personal cosmetics," the girl volunteered.

Shower bags in hand, we boarded the golf cart and she dropped us at the spa in a couple of minutes. "Call me when you're ready to go back." She smiled and gave a little wave.

In my days as a corporate executive, traveling on an expense account, I stayed in some fine hotels, but I've never had a better shower than that one, nor one in a nicer facility. The private stall and dressing area was marble, the plumbing fixtures gold-plated. When I stepped out of the shower after an extended stay, there was an attendant with an endless supply of fresh, hot towels. After I was dressed, I sat in the lounge area reading yachting magazines while I waited for Leslie. She appeared in a few minutes, looking fresh and relaxed. "Let's walk back, okay?" she asked.

"Okay," I agreed. "How was your shower?"

"$75, at least," she said. "How about yours?"

"Huh?"

"What?" she asked.

"I don't get the $75."

"In hindsight, I would have been willing to pay at least that much for that shower. I haven't felt this clean in months; especially my hair."

I nodded. The price of dockage suddenly seemed much less exorbitant. Still, we left the next day before checkout time. We couldn't afford to become accustomed to living that way.

****

The places in the Bahamas that we enjoyed most were the small, out-of-the-way villages. The few times that we happened to be the only boat in one of those spots, we found the people to be warm, friendly, and generous. We spent some memorable hours sitting in the shade visiting, listening to tales of lives mostly untouched by the tourist trade that is the Bahamas' main source of income. All the low, sandy islands had lovely, unspoiled beaches lapped by clear, warm water, even if the island itself was desert-like, which most were.

We have fond memories of some of those tiny villages. It was in the shade of an abandoned, open-air market in one of them that an older fellow told us about his experiences as a fishing guide.

"I always know how to fish," he told us. "When I was a child, to eat, you must catch fish. One day when I was a young man, I was wading, fishing on the flats, and this man in a dinghy came from one of those big sport-fishing boats. He talk to me 'bout the fishing for a while, and then he ask me to come with them, show them how to catch the fish. I went with them for some weeks, on that big boat. I take them to the places I know, and we catch many fish. I had a fine bed on that boat, and they fed me what they ate, and gave me beer to drink with them. It was some good living, easy living. When they have to leave, they say, 'Willie, how much do we owe you?' At first, I don't know what they mean. They talk some more, and I see that they mean to pay me for show them how to fish, where to fish."

He paused, taking a sip of water from a recycled rum bottle, his eyes on the horizon, looking into the past.

"So I say, 'No, you don't must pay me. You give me my living these weeks. We fish. Is what I do.' The man, he shake his head, and he say, 'Willie, I take care of you, my friend.' He write down my name in his book, and they give me some beer to take home. I like those people; I say to them I will miss them. Some weeks later, I walk by the post office, and the man at the post office come out and say that someone is sending me money. It is the man from the boat, and he has done something with the bank so every month, I get some money. He is a rich man, I t'ink. Every month this money comes, still now, years passed. And then, not so long after they leave, another sport-fishing boat come. The man from the other boat, he tell them, 'Look for Willie. He fish wit' you.' So for many years, I am a fishing guide. They pay me; the man, he still pay me every month."

"That sounds like a good living, Willie," I said.

"It is my living, fishing. I don't spend that money, much. I don't need money. The sea and the island, they give me everyt'ing I need."

"What about fruit? Vegetables? You spend some money for those, don't you?" Leslie asked.

He shook his head. "No, ma'am. I grow some."

"I thought there wasn't enough water and the soil was too poor, Willie," I said.

"That's what the government men in Nassau say," Willie agreed. "You come to my house, now. I show you they are wrong."

Willie led us to his house, modest enough, even by island standards, but comfortable and clean.

"My wife is not home," he observed, leading us around back.

We were surprised to see lush fruit trees growing out of cracks and small holes in the jagged limestone.

"Where do you get the water," I asked. Willie responded by putting a hand on my shoulder and leading me around behind the small rise in the limestone where one tree stood. He kneeled down and traced one of the tree's roots along a crack that disappeared into a deep crevasse.

"Water down there," he said.

"But isn't it salt?" I asked, conscious that we stood only a few feet above sea level.

He shook his head, leading me to a large, deep hole in the limestone. It was about two feet across at the surface and followed a crooked path down that blocked our view of the bottom. Willie picked up an empty one-gallon paint can with a light rope tied to the bail and tossed it down the hole. After it bounced down the hole, banging its way out of sight, we heard a splash. He pulled on the line, retrieving the paint can, now full of water.

"Sweet water," he said, scooping a handful out of the can and tasting it. I dipped a hand in and tried it. It was, as he said, 'sweet.' It had a slight brackish taste, but it was much better than the water from the tap in George Town.

"Where does it come from," I asked.

He shrugged. "The Lord gives us what we need. I'm sorry the fruit isn't in season, but let me give you some vegetables." He gathered up a beautiful head of cabbage and several cucumbers, picking as we walked. When we reached his front gate, he handed them to us, saying, "Thank you for visiting. I hope you'll come again, now you know where I live."

Back to Florida

We left Nassau at about 9:00 a.m. Since we planned to sail non-stop all the way to Florida, there was no need to rush our departure, as we would be traveling for a day and a half to two days, depending on the conditions we found on the way. We took a comfortable angle on the wind, holding a course that took us around the east side of the Berry Islands, where we fell off a bit to the west, following the Northwest Providence Channel, the deep-water route to Florida. It's several miles wide, although until sundown we could see the low, scattered Berry Islands on our port side and the larger bulk of Grand Bahama Island to our starboard. We had cruise ships and freighters for company during our night watches; studying their navigation lights to ensure that we would stay clear of them kept the person on watch alert. By daylight the following morning, we left West End, the town on the western tip of Grand Bahama, astern as we laid a straight-line course to the Fort Pierce Inlet.

We were in the Gulf Stream once again, but this time it was favoring us. We were crossing at an angle to the axis of the current with the bow pointed away from the flow, so we gained a couple of knots as we left the Bahamas well behind us. We worked out an appropriate course adjustment to avoid making our Florida landfall too far to the north, and settled in to admire the indigo blue water in the bright sunlight. Because we weren't fighting the current on this crossing, we had a much smoother ride, and we were much more attuned to the beauty of this amazing phenomenon. The water in the Stream is a different shade of blue from the rest of the surrounding water; it's such an intense, dark hue that it's almost purple. It's also much warmer than the water in which we had been sailing for the last few weeks. We turned on the sea water tap at the galley sink and immediately knew we had entered the stream, just from the warmth of the water. Crossing with the current in daylight was much more interesting than crossing against the current in the dark had been.

The trip was progressing so well that we discussed changing our plans and heading for Charleston or Beaufort, bypassing Florida, but we decided to stick with our original plan. We were low on groceries, and there were a number of small but irritating problems with the boat that we had not been able to fix in the Bahamas because there were no parts to be found there. It made more sense to spend a little time in Florida sorting things out. Besides, it was still early April. Although we were sailing in bathing suits, it was a bit early in the season to head for the mid-Atlantic coast. We didn't want to get cold, and we had not studied the offshore weather expected for the next few days. Off the Carolina coast in the Gulf Stream wasn't a good place to be if a late cold front blew through with strong northerly winds. High winds opposing the swift current would make for a vicious sea state. We knew that we could reach Fort Pierce in just a few more hours.

By late afternoon, we had the coast of Florida in sight, and as the sun began to set we spotted the outermost buoy of the Fort Pierce entrance channel. As we approached the channel entrance in the fading light, a pod of dolphins came to welcome us home. "They probably work for the Fort Pierce Chamber of Commerce," Leslie quipped, as she scrambled forward to the bowsprit to applaud them. During the dolphin show, we enjoyed a spectacular sunset directly off our bow. As the pastel hue faded from the water ahead of us, a full moon rose behind us, changing the light from soft pink to a bright, cool white for the finale of the dolphins' performance. The channel was easy to follow; it was well-marked and lighted for commercial shipping. Once we were inside the inlet, we worked our way into the familiar anchorage where we had spent a couple of nights on our way south.

When we were settled, I called U.S. Customs on our cell phone to announce our arrival. They granted us clearance over the phone, issuing a clearance number to enter in the ship's log. I can't count the number of times that I returned to the U.S. from abroad during my work-related travels, but certainly none of those arrivals felt as much like a homecoming as this one did. Tired after almost 40 hours underway, we heated a can of soup for supper and almost fell asleep before we finished it.

The next morning, we slept in until about eight o'clock. After coffee and breakfast, we retrieved the anchor and followed the Waterway north for a few hours to the Vero Beach Marina.

****

We were in no hurry to leave Vero Beach this time. We took care of our boat repairs and stocked the pantry, indulging ourselves in the things we had missed. We both were craving potato chips, which had been unavailable in most of the places we had been. We could have bought them in Nassau, but they were about four times as expensive as they were in the U.S. Besides the chips, Leslie satisfied her sweet tooth with chocolate and I enjoyed plenty of ice-cold beer. Chocolate had been generally unavailable where we had been. Beer was plentiful in the Bahamas, and could be found in the smallest of villages, but it was about $50 per case for the run-of-the-mill brands, and more for the premium labels.

We visited again with Leslie's aunt and uncle and talked to all our relatives on the telephone as often and for as long as we wanted. We had several months' worth of mail forwarded to the marina and we spent a few days sorting through it. We found a number of things that required our attention, not the least of which was our federal income tax return. We had managed to find someone in George Town who had a copy of the form to request an extension of time to file, and we had made a photocopy of it and sent it in, but it was relief to get the paperwork done and the taxes filed.

Studying the statements from our brokerage accounts occupied us for a while. We had a general sense that the stock market had been in decline while we were away; we would periodically hear a newscast that included the Dow's recent close, but until we saw the statements, we had no idea what effect that had on our mostly well-diversified portfolio. We were a little disappointed to see our current net worth; we still felt comfortable enough, but the drop in value was sobering.

Re-entry

We stayed in Vero Beach for almost a month, enjoying the easy access to all the things we had missed and waiting for the weather to get warmer up north. We planned to spend the summer in the Annapolis area; from there, we could take a commuter bus to Washington, D.C. Once in Washington, the Metro system would enable us to visit our old neighborhood. We needed to see our dentist and take care of some banking business, and we wanted to visit the warehouse where we had stored the remains of our life ashore. We had done a decent job of guessing what we would need on the boat, but with a year of experience, we saw that some refinement was in order. We had taken a number of things with us that did nothing but occupy precious space.

Between Vero Beach and Titusville, *Play Actor's* engine overheated. That had been one of the persistent problems that we thought we had fixed in Vero Beach. This sort of problem had seemed much more intimidating in the Bahamas, where there were no part suppliers ready to hand, and often there was no one for miles around to offer help if we needed it. When the temperature gauge pegged a few miles south of Titusville, we found a wide spot in the Waterway and anchored several hundred yards from the main channel, safely out of the way. As we waited for the engine to cool down enough so that I could work on it, we began to realize that the reason we had found problems like this intimidating in the Bahamas had more to do with the unfamiliar surroundings than with any actual increase in danger.

The problem was identical, whether we confronted it in unfamiliar waters or 'at home.' The consequences varied depending on where we were, as did the available solutions. Wherever this particular failure happened, the immediate result would be that we couldn't use the engine to move the boat. If this had occurred in the Bahamas, we would have been in relatively open water with a good breeze, so we would have had the option of sailing to overcome our difficulty. Help and spare parts might be far away, but we had a way to reach them that wasn't available to us ten miles south of Titusville. The waters were too confined there for sailing to be a practical solution. Near Titusville, though, help of all sorts was only a phone call away. In a few minutes, we could have a towboat alongside to take us to a nearby repair facility. In our case, we recognized, that was an illusory comfort. To avail ourselves of those services would be costly, in terms of both money and our self-esteem.

Part of the attraction of the cruising life to us was the opportunity for self-sufficiency. The boat that had once been our weekend getaway had become our self-contained world; we could take all our belongings and support systems with us, anywhere and anytime we chose to move. This appeared to provide a great deal more control over life's vicissitudes than living ashore, but we were learning that it really just made our lives subject to unforeseen disruptions of a different sort.

In my early childhood, when I went fishing with my father, we ventured off in small boats, sometimes not much bigger than *Play Actor's* dinghy. We would spend days without seeing another boat. In those days, there were no cell phones and ship-to-shore radios were not available for small boats. There were no towboats to call if the engine failed or you ran aground, and there were no electronic gizmos to tell you where you were. Of course, as a small boy, I wasn't troubled by any of that. My father was there to deal with any problems, and he did so often and with a great deal of resourcefulness and confidence.

As I grew up, I absorbed the reality that when you left the shore behind, you were on your own. Your safety and comfort were in your own hands, and you dealt with whatever situation arose as best you could with the resources you had available. Because of those experiences, my approach to boating was an anachronism in the modern day. In equipping a boat, my first priorities were for self-sufficiency and redundancy, but in an ancient sense. You never set out without plenty of food and water because you never knew how long you might be gone. I had that driven home at the age of six when my father and I came upon two men in a small boat, one delirious and the other not far from it; they had forgotten to bring drinking water, and had been exposed to the heat and humidity for over 12 hours. We gave them a quart of water and watched as they recovered before our eyes. "What about water for us, Papa?" I had asked, worried, after we left the grateful men to find their way home. "That's why we always carry more than we need," he said. "Never fail to help somebody in trouble," he continued. "One day you may be the one who needs help."

We had the spare parts, tools, and know-how to repair any essential equipment aboard *Play Actor*, even if 'know-how' sometimes took the form of repair manuals, which we assiduously acquired anytime we added a new piece of equipment. If research or experience indicated that we might not be able to fix an important piece of equipment if it broke, we had a backup for it, or a plan to do without it.

When the engine cooled down sufficiently, I went to work rebuilding the coolant pumps; Leslie passed me tools and dug the parts out of our spares locker. Once I had the pumps apart, I saw the problem. One of the new parts that I had installed during the rebuild in Vero Beach had failed, probably from a manufacturing defect. As I put the pump back together with a new replacement part, Leslie said, "Glad we had the part."

It was a soft rubber impeller, a part prone to wear and failure. We normally kept several aboard. "How many are left in the box?" I asked.

A moment later, Leslie said, "None. That's the last one. Think we can find more in Daytona?"

"Yep. Even if we have to order them from somewhere," I said. "We're gonna put a lot of hours on the engine between here and Annapolis. Gotta have spare impellers."

We discovered that there were no impellers in stock in Daytona, so we ordered several to be shipped in. That gave us a couple of days to explore Daytona Beach. It was familiar to me from my college days at the University of Florida, just a little over an hour away by car, but I hadn't been there in 30 years and it was completely new to Leslie. The famed beach looked decidedly disappointing after the endless unoccupied stretches of clean, white sand that we had left in the Bahamas. Of course, nobody drives on the beaches there, either. Seeing the automobile traffic on Daytona Beach was another reminder that there's no place like home...

Back to the Chesapeake

We spent close to a month going north from Florida to the Chesapeake, pausing only when necessary. We had enjoyed the trip south, but the northbound trip was more tedious. We knew our way; we knew where to find places to anchor, and we knew where to get the things we needed, but for much of the trip north, the weather was hot and still. The swampy areas that had charmed us on our way south were hot, sticky, and bug-infested. We were relieved to get to Norfolk and the more open, breezier waters of the Chesapeake Bay.

We stayed in Norfolk for a few days, enjoying the city and doing a little shopping for clothing. After spending the winter in a sub-tropical climate, we found the need to adjust our wardrobe. The cotton polo shirts that we had both been happily wearing on the boat for years were far too heavy to be comfortable; we found lightweight, short-sleeved cotton shirts on sale and bought several apiece, retiring the knitted cotton shirts to the rag bag. They made fine polishing cloths.

We retraced our steps up the Bay, stopping for a day's rest in St. Mary's City to see what progress had been made on the archaeological sites. The night before we planned to leave for Solomon's Island, a violent thunderstorm blew through the area, and we suffered a direct lightning strike to the top of our aluminum mast. We had been counting the seconds between the lightning flashes and the thunder for a few minutes, calculating the distance of each strike as the storm drew ever closer. It was early in the season for this sort of weather, and we didn't remember hearing anything about thunderstorms in the forecast. I was reaching to turn on the radio for an updated forecast when the cabin was filled with blinding white light accompanied by a deafening crash. I was reminded of the effect of a stun-grenade from my military training.

A bit dazed, we noticed that all our lights were out, and we both smelled smoke. We grabbed flashlights and started looking for the source of the smoke, quickly isolating it to a piece of electronic equipment in the battery charging system. Satisfied that we didn't have a fire, our next immediate concern was the watertight integrity of the hull; when the energy of a lightning bolt comes into a boat, it doesn't stay. It usually exits below the waterline, sometimes taking parts of the hull with it, particularly through-hull drains and water intake fittings, made of bronze and normally tied to the boat's electrical system to help control electrolytic corrosion, an ever present problem with metal parts around salt water. We checked the through-hull fittings first and then scanned the rest of the interior below the waterline. We weren't sinking, and we weren't on fire. We were both well, our hearing and vision quickly returning to normal.

We breathed a sigh of relief and began methodically checking the electrical system and the electronics. The light bulbs which had been on at the time of the strike were destroyed, but the others survived. We turned on enough of them to see what we were doing as we went on with our evaluation. The main components of the electrical system all worked, but none of the sensitive electronics were functional. We cranked the engine, relieved when it started; we had worried about damage to the electric starting circuit. As the diesel rumbled, we noticed that there was no alternator output; we couldn't charge the batteries from the engine. That was not an immediate problem, but we needed to be careful about our use of electricity until we fixed it. Shaken by our close call but relieved that we escaped with relatively minor damage, we shut off the engine and went to bed.

The next morning I started to make coffee, only to realize that our inverter, which allowed us to run household electrical appliances from our batteries, wouldn't work. Our coffee grinder was silent, and we had to make do with instant coffee. By the time we finished breakfast it was late enough to call our insurance company and report the damages. They assured us that there would be no problem with coverage, and hung up to make arrangements with a boatyard in Solomon's Island to haul the boat out the next morning for an inspection by a marine surveyor to confirm our initial assessment that the hull was intact. They also arranged for a rigger to go aloft and examine the mast and the rigging, and for a survey of the electrical system. They called back a little later to give us the particulars, and we left for Solomon's Island.

We spent several days there; after the inspection, we began replacing the damaged electronics, finding most of what we needed in the local marine supply stores and ordering the rest. Our top priority was the inverter; we missed our freshly ground coffee. By mid-July, we had everything back in order, and we sailed north to Annapolis where we planned to spend the balance of the summer.

We spent July and August doing all the things we had planned to do while close to our old home. We divided our time among a number of familiar spots within a day's sail of Annapolis, using it as a base of sorts while we worked out what we wanted to do next. We saw the dentist and the doctor; Leslie got new glasses. We added a few things to our stored goods in Alexandria, Virginia, and took care of our banking business. Our daughter had finished graduate school and had spent the summer working in Paris as a bicycle tour guide. She came and stayed with us for a few days before reporting to work at her first 'real' job in Dallas.

Through all this, we watched the stock market and the value of our nest egg continue the decline which had started while we were in the Bahamas. Several of the folks that we had met during the last year were in the area; we would see them from time to time. One by one, the other couples began to put their boats on the market and look for jobs, their cruising plans abruptly terminated. The long term prospects for the economy looked gloomy in the wake of the dot-com meltdown, and we were continually analyzing our own financial situation.

When we had embarked on our adventure, we had expected to be able to live reasonably well on investment income. When I reached normal retirement age in 15 years, we expected that our nest egg could begin to grow again as we began to live on my pensions and social security. It was evident based on the market's recent performance that we would have to spend some of our principal, at least for a while, but we thought we could make it.

We considered going back to work, which was not something we had planned to do. While employment prospects were generally dim, I had been self-employed for several years before we left, providing general and financial management expertise to small high-tech companies. I still had fresh connections with enough people so that I could have probably gotten work, especially as I had skills that were more demand in hard times than good times. Leslie had a sterling track record in retail management, having most recently taken a large women's clothing store from a bleak situation to profitability. Her old employer would no doubt be happy to put her in another troubled store.

The problem with all that was that neither of us could imagine going back to that life. To do so meant making a commitment of years; years during which we couldn't sail when we wanted or call our time our own. We decided that we would prefer to live more frugally and keep to our plan. Initially, we had found it strange to always be in each other's company, but we had quickly adjusted to that, and we didn't like the prospect of going back to work and enduring extended periods of separation. We had encountered a lot of extraordinarily happy people over the last year, and none of them had much money. The things that we enjoyed most – time alone together, the natural beauty of the ocean and the coastal environment, meeting interesting people, and observing wildlife in its natural habitat – didn't involve spending money.

Our new life was hard work; we had not expected that. We had both remarked over the last year that we had never worked as hard for money as we had worked for the past year. To keep the boat going and just to live was more stressful and physically demanding than we had ever imagined, but the results were inherently satisfying. The stress that we encountered now could be dealt with by taking concrete, direct action, unlike the stress we had known before. We were healthier, more fit, and happier than we had ever been. We reasoned that we could always work for money if we had to; we were both well-educated and we both had a broad range of marketable skills. We decided to focus on reining in our spending habits so that we could keep doing what we enjoyed most.

Committed to continue our cruising life, at least for the moment, we settled in Annapolis to take care of a few last-minute boat projects. It was early September, and there were just a few things that we needed to do before we set off on another winter adventure; we were beginning to discuss where we might go for the coming winter, but the larger question of our finances had occupied our attention until now. We would spend a week or two in Annapolis getting the boat and ourselves ready while we thought about where to go. I had a dentist appointment in Virginia in a couple of days, so we needed a quick project. We still hadn't replaced our stereo that was destroyed in the lightning strike. It had been an expensive, marine-grade piece of equipment. We were more careful with our money now, so we planned to go to a big chain electronics store at the Annapolis Mall and buy a mid-range car stereo, which would meet our needs well enough at a fraction of what we had paid for the unit we were replacing.

We got an early start, intending to be there when the store opened, so we could get back and install the stereo that afternoon. We landed our dinghy at a dock adjacent to the Naval Academy that we often used, walked up to the State House, and caught a bus to the mall. We walked into the store about five minutes after it opened, to find the entire staff gathered in front of a huge television, watching what we took to be a movie.

Thinking that they were just concluding a meeting of some sort, we hung back, waiting for them to finish. We were idly watching whatever was on television, although we couldn't hear the sound very well. We recognized the Manhattan skyline, and there was a close up of wreckage, with smoke pouring from a damaged building. As the camera zoomed out, we recognized the World Trade Center just as the second plane struck the tower. We still thought we were watching a movie, and were remarking to one another on the amazing special effects, when someone changed the channel and turned up the volume. We heard the latest on the terrorist attacks from CNN. Stunned, we were trying to process what we had seen when the power in the mall shut off abruptly.

As the emergency exit lighting flickered on, we were escorted out of the store into the mall itself, where a crowd of alarmed people milled around. Before we got our bearings, there was an announcement on the public address system to the effect that the Governor of Maryland had declared a state of emergency. All businesses were directed to close immediately, and people should make their way home as expeditiously as possible. We left the mall, wondering if the buses would be running, knowing that if necessary, we could walk back to the boat in 90 minutes or so.

The buses were running and our timing was good. We caught one almost immediately and we were soon back on the waterfront downtown. I glanced at my watch, noticing that we had been gone for less than an hour. When we reached the Naval Academy, we didn't recognize it. The entrances had been barricaded with sections of heavy concrete wall about four feet high, placed in an overlapping zigzag pattern, so that to drive in, a vehicle would have to back up and turn sharply several times. Marines in full battle gear manned heavy machine guns at each fortified gate, and stood guard every few feet around the perimeter.

One sentry was standing by the ladder to the dinghy dock where our rowing dinghy was bobbing quietly. I approached him and offered a quick explanation of our intentions, at which he nodded and stepped back, watching us sternly as we unlocked our little boat and returned to *Play Actor*. We spent the day listening to the news along with the rest of America, glad that we had a transistor radio as a backup to the broken stereo. From a local station, we learned that the power failure at the mall had been a pure coincidence, which was a great relief to us, but that was the only good news we heard on September 11, 2001.

And Then Again

As the U.S. began to grasp what had happened, we, like most Americans, assessed the impact of the attack on our lives. Our family was lucky; we had no one lost or injured. Our son was beginning a career as a U.S. Marine, though, and we were worried about that. Our daughter had called us several times, quite shaken by the images on television of the plane protruding from the side of the Pentagon. For the 14 years that we had been in the D. C. area, we had lived in a 12-storey condominium building just across the expressway from the Pentagon. My normal daily run had taken me within a hundred yards of the point of impact, and she and I had run that route together countless times; I understood her feelings.

As we sorted through our collective and individual reactions to what had happened, Leslie and I continued our preparations for another winter afloat. It was beginning to get cold, and we were committed to going south again. We had been thinking about going to the Caribbean; a return to the Bahamas didn't appeal to us. We were glad we had seen them, but we had no desire to spend more time there. Unsettled by the terrorist attack and the uncertainty surrounding our nation's response, we decided that this was not the time for us to venture far from home. We felt a need to be available to family in this time of unrest, and all last winter we had been cut off from even telephone contact.

There were places along the Waterway where we had wanted to spend more time, and we also wanted to visit the Florida Keys. The Caribbean would still be there in a year or two, and we were more convinced every day that we would do whatever we needed to in order to continue to live the way we had for the last year; for all the irritations and surprises, it had been a wonderful year, so we left Annapolis in late September for another run down the Ditch. In answer to that pampered-looking woman who had asked us in Myrtle Beach almost a year ago, "What kind of life is that," we would now say, "Our Life's a Ditch, and we wouldn't have it any other way."

Epilogue

We did explore the Florida Keys during the winter of 2001-2002. We spent more time in Charleston and Miami, as well, until we began to feel at home in both places. We continued to poke along the Waterway for two more seasons after that, until it became our neighborhood, in effect. Each year, we moved south from the Chesapeake as the leaves began to turn, trying to time our trip to stay just ahead of winter. We began to recognize and enjoy more and more of our neighbors, both the ones who lived and worked along the shoreline, and the ones who migrated with the seasons. We never took the Waterway north in the warm weather again, though. One trip like that was enough.

Instead, we would wait in Miami until the cold fronts began to moderate. When we had a week's forecast without a front, we would sail out into the Gulf Stream, working our way to the eastern wall. We had learned that most of the squalls and thunderstorms that came off the North American continent stopped or at least dissipated substantially in the eastern part of the Stream. With the favorable current from the Gulf Stream and a warm southerly breeze, we usually made Beaufort, North Carolina, in three or four days of beautiful, round-the-clock ocean sailing, catching fish for dinner and admiring the endless array of stars at night, with no light from land to dull heaven's luster.

In the spring of 2004, on our 20th wedding anniversary, we were sailing in the moonlight 100 miles off the coast of South Carolina, heading north for the summer. During a point in our watch schedule when we were both awake, we discussed what we would like to do on our 25th anniversary. Two things that we both wanted were to spend more time in the open ocean and to see the islands of the Eastern Caribbean. In the fall of 2004, we took the Ditch as far south as Beaufort, North Carolina, where we sailed out into the North Atlantic, steering on an imaginary point about 200 miles south of Bermuda. From there we turned south and rode the trade winds *Dungda de Islan'*, but that's another book, and if you read it, you'll learn where we spent our 25th anniversary.

Thanks for joining us,

Bud and Leslie Dougherty

A Note from the Author

Thank you for reading **Life's a Ditch**. Readers are the most important participants in the book business, and I appreciate your investment in my work. I hope you enjoyed it, and I welcome your comments or questions. Just send me an email at clrd@clrdougherty.com, and I'll be pleased to answer. If you enjoyed this book, you would probably enjoy **Dungda de Islan'**, which relates our adventures as we sailed from North Carolina to the British Virgin Islands and began cruising the Caribbean. Links to **Dungda de Islan'** and my other books are on the last page of this book.

About the Author

Charles Dougherty wrote quite a bit of fiction before publishing **Deception in Savannah**, his first novel. Most of his earlier fiction works took the form of business plans, written to secure funding for projects and startup ventures during his corporate and consulting work, but he put all of that behind him when he wrote **Deception in Savannah,** a tongue-in-cheek crime novel.

Since **Deception in Savannah** was published, he has written a number of other books. **Bluewater Killer, Bluewater Vengeance, Bluewater Voodoo, Bluewater Ice,** and **Bluewater Betrayal** are the first five books in his **Bluewater Thriller** series. The **Bluewater Thrillers** are set in the yachting world of the Caribbean and chronicle the adventures of two young women running a luxury charter yacht in a rough-and-tumble environment. Book six of the **Bluewater Thriller** series will be published in 2014. Besides the Bluewater Thrillers, he wrote **Twisted Love**, a psycho-thriller, and **Deception in Savannah**, a character-driven crime novel with some humorous twists.

He has also written two non-fiction books. **Life's a Ditch** is the story of how he and his wife moved aboard their sailboat, *Play Actor*, and their adventures along the east coast of the U.S. **Dungda de Islan'** relates their experiences while cruising the Caribbean.

He resides with his wife aboard *Play Actor*, sailing wherever their fancy and the trade winds take them.

Other Books by C.L.R. Dougherty

Fiction:

Deception in Savannah

Bluewater Killer

Bluewater Vengeance

Bluewater Voodoo

Bluewater Ice

Bluewater Betrayal

Twisted Love

Short Story:

The Lost Tourist Franchise

Non-fiction:

Dungda de Islan'

Life's a Ditch

For more information, please visit:

http://www.clrdougherty.com or
http://amazon.com/author/clrdougherty

28108870R00128

Made in the USA
Lexington, KY
05 December 2013